Understanding The Twelve Tribes

Boundaries & Surrounding Nations

MENASHE HAR-EL

cartaJerusalem

First published in 2018 by
CARTA Jerusalem

11 Rivka Street, P.O.B. 2500,
Jerusalem 9102401, Israel
E-mail: carta@carta.co.il
www.carta-jerusalem.com

Quotations from the Hebrew Bible follow the King James Version unless otherwise indicated.

Great care has been taken to establish sources of illustrations. If inadvertently we omitted to do so, due credit will be given in the next edition.

ISBN: 978-965-220-894-1

Printed in the United States of America

CONTENTS

LIST OF MAPS

THE FAMILY OF NATIONS

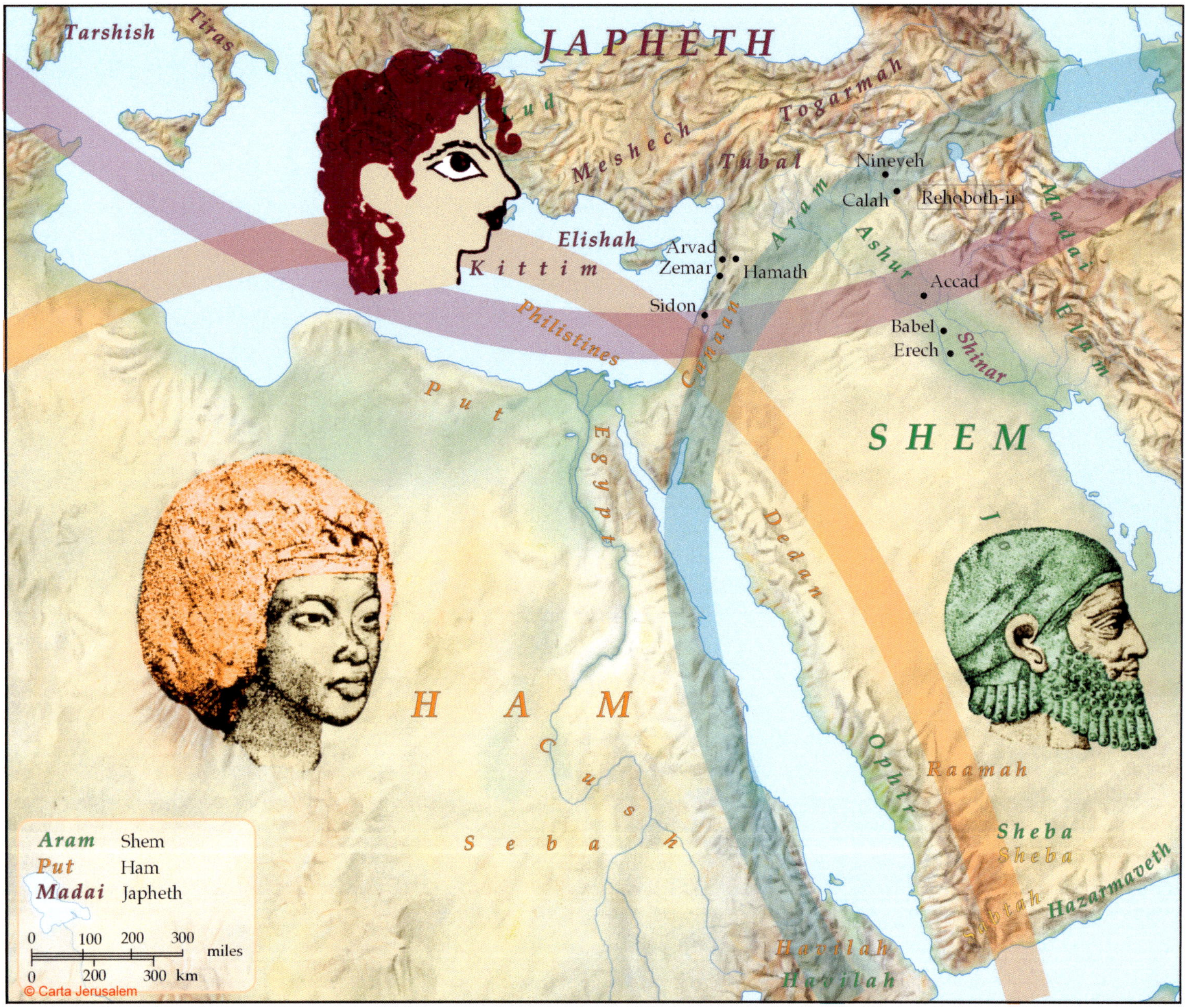

(Genesis 10)

INTRODUCTION

The biblical world extended in the east from Ophir, apparently the Malaysian islands in Southeast Asia, and India (Genesis, ch. 10; Esther 1:1; I Chronicles 1:23, etc.); via Persia and Medes, Tubal and Meshech south of the Black Sea (Ezekiel 27:13, 32:26, etc.); to Togarmah (Anatolia; Ezekiel 27:14, 38:6), Elishah-Kittim (Cyprus), Greece and Tarshish—which was either Sardinia or Spain—in the west (Ezekiel 27:6–7, 27:12; Jonah 1:3); and north to south from Anatolia to Cush and Sheba in Ethiopia, and Arabia; and Put, in North Africa (Jeremiah 46:9; Ezekiel 27:10, etc.). Thus Canaan, the Land of Israel, was situated in the middle of the countries of the biblical world and served as a bridge between them.

Egyptian and Mesopotamian sources tell us of the countries on the borders of Canaan in biblical times. They were well-defined; in biblical terms, "from the river of Egypt to the great river, the river Euphrates" (Genesis 15:18). Those borders stretched from the Mediterranean in the west to the desert east of the Jordan, and from the river of Egypt—apparently the Pelusian branch east of the Nile, or the El-Arish wadi—in the southwest; from the inhabited Negeb mountains to Kadesh-barnea in the south; from Mount Hor in northern Lebanon to Lebo-hamath near the city of Hamma in Syria in the north; northward through the Bashan region to Aram-damascus in the northeast; and in the east along the Jordan rift, the Sea of Galilee, the Dead Sea and the Arabah, and Ammon, Moab and Edom (Numbers 34:2–12).

It should be noted that the country is longitudinally divided; the Mediterranean in the west and the Syrian and Arabian deserts in the east, with an emphasis on the *four corners* where the major neighboring nations lived: Egypt in the southwest, Sidon and the Hittites in the northwest, Aram-damascus in the northeast, and Edom in the southeast. The country was vulnerable from the military and economic standpoints at these "corners," for it was there that the international highways met.

Ten nations of different racial and religious origins lived in Canaan (Genesis 15:18–21). Furthermore, the country's variegated physical structure contributed to many political entities and in Canaanite times no one ruler ever ruled over the entire country. These divisions and the country's location at international crossroads made it prone to the invasion of the great regional empires: the nearby Egyptians in the south and the somewhat farther Mesopotamians in the north.

Canaan extended over the Land of Israel and western Syria and served both as a bridge and a barrier between the major cultures of the ancient Middle East. The region's great powers continuously tried to weaken the Canaanite nations so that they might subjugate them at will, and they carried on a policy of divide and conquer. The Egyptians forced the Canaanites to pay an annual worker head tax, and made them repair the commercial caravan routes and supply the Egyptian armies that crossed the country at frequent intervals. The only time Canaan enjoyed tranquility was when the great powers were weak. Even without the threat of the great powers, during times of distress and famine, or when the Canaanite peoples fought against each other, the country was prone to invasion from the east by the nomadic tribes who would pillage them or shepherd their flocks on the ruins of their settlements. As if this was not enough, Canaan was also open to the invasion of the Sea Peoples.

The Philistines, who invaded the country from Crete, exploited the Egyptian withdrawal from Canaan to settle there and seize the rich agricultural grain-growing areas of what would later be known as the Judean southern coastal plain and lowlands (Joshua 13:2–3). The Philistines eventually assimilated into the Canaanites and even worshiped the Canaanite god Dagon in Ashdod and Gaza (I Samuel, chapter 5; Judges 16:23). At that time the Tyrians and Sidonians controlled the northern coast of Canaan, and the Israelites conquered the inland and mountain regions on both sides of the Jordan. When Joshua conquered the land, including the thirty-one Canaanite royal cities (Joshua 12:9–24), it was at a time of intense division among the Canaanite peoples. Now weakened, some Canaanite peoples were restricted to the Phoenician border area while others assimilated into the Israelite tribes.

The Israelite colonization after the Exodus began in the mountains east of the Jordan and in the areas of Judah bordering the desert and the northern Negeb. The Israelite tribes initially lived a seminomadic existence as shepherds; later they settled permanently in all regions of mountain and desert agriculture (Numbers 32:16; Joshua 20:8–9). Since the country was then surrounded or isolated by the Israelites in the south and east, the conquest under Joshua prepared the ground for the inclusion of the western part of the country, as well. Later, the major Israelite tribes came to control the most important regions of the country. *Judah* took over the *Negeb* and *Judea* and the tribal portions of Benjamin and Dan on the coastal plain, the portion of Simeon in the southwestern Negeb and the territory of the sub-Judean clans of the Calebites, Kenites and Jerahmeelites in the southern part of the Judean Hills (I Samuel 27:10, 30:14). The tribe of *Manasseh* gained control over *Samaria* and Ephraim's portion in the south of the region, as well as *Gilead* and *Bashan* in the northeast. *Gad* colonized Ammon and Moab and Reuben's allotment in the southern part of Transjordan. *Naphtali* settled in Galilee and the portions of Asher, Zebulun and Issachar, and the northeastern portion of Dan.

THE GEOGRAPHICAL REGIONS OF THE LAND

THE GEOGRAPHICAL DIVISION OF THE LAND AMONG THE TRIBES AT THE TIME OF JOSHUA

(Joshua 13–19)

Joshua divided the Land of Israel, on both sides of the Jordan, into twelve tribal portions which were territorially fairly well-defined. We will now discuss the significance of the tribes in Bible times, and examine the borders of the tribal portions from the viewpoint of geographical boundaries between them, and assess their nature and importance.

The remains at Shiloh (photo Samuel Magal).

The Nature of the Tribes of Israel

The tribe was the traditional social unit of the nomads and seminomadic groups among the Semitic peoples, such as the Amorites, the Arameans and others. The Bible contains numerous references to the tribes of Israel even before they settled in the Promised Land. The tribe was divided into four units: the tribe as a whole; the clan, headed by the chieftain (Numbers 34:17–29); the family (Exodus 6:14; Numbers 2:34); and the household (I Samuel 9:21, 10:19–21).

The consolidation of the tribes took place at the Giving of the Law at Mount Sinai in the wilderness of Sinai, and in the Negeb. The physical conditions of the desert molded their character and strengthened the bonds between the tribes and their chiefs (Genesis 36:15; Exodus 34:31; Numbers 1:16). The chief was responsible for the organization of the tribe and the provision of basic needs, such as water supplies, pastures and security. It was also his concern to maintain the values, morals and religious precepts of the social group. Mutual help was one of the main precepts of the tribe.

The changeover from a nomadic and seminomadic existence to permanent settlement was a process that united the formerly disconnected tribes into one people living together in its land with its own king. The links included blood relationships, religious ideology and national destiny.

The Tribal and Ritual Alliance

Joshua, Moses' military commander, conducted several wars before the tribes entered the land to the west of the Jordan, at a time when the outcome of the battle determined control over the main roads of each region. The first battle was with Amalek at Rephidim near Egypt, on the Way of the Wilderness in Sinai (Exodus 17:9–13), resulting in victory over the enemy. The second campaign was against an allied force of Amalekites of the Negeb, Amorites and Canaanites at Kadesh-barnea on the Way of Shur leading to Beer-sheba, which resulted in defeat for the Israelites (Numbers 14:40–45). The third battle was against the king of Arad who dwelt in the Negeb, on the Way of Atharim leading to the Judean Hills. Here, too, the Israelites were defeated and forced to retreat (Numbers 21:1). The fourth war was between the Israelites and Sihon king of the Amorites from the mountains of Moab, and the fifth against Og king of Bashan, who controlled the King's Highway which leads east of the Jordan and Damascus, both resulting in victory for the Israelites (Numbers 21:21–35).

After these campaigns, the Israelites were able to settle at the southern border of Judah, in the wildernesses of the northern and central Negeb, and in the semidesert areas of the mountains to the east of the Jordan. At first they were seminomadic herdsmen, later becoming settled farmers combining livestock rearing with agriculture in the mountain wilderness. Their penetration into these regions facilitated the entry of the Israelites into the land of Canaan in the next stage of their history. They were able to conquer the land since it was surrounded by Israelite tribes to the south and east, and the roads entering and leaving it were also under Israelite control.

During the period of Israelite penetration into the land to the west of the Jordan, an alliance was made between several of the tribes' ritual centers that were set up, Joshua building an altar to the Twelve Tribes of Israel at *Gilgal*, near Jericho (Joshua 4:19–22), where he allocated the territories of Judah, Ephraim and Manasseh (Joshua 15–17). Gilgal remained a ritual center into the time of Saul and his wars with Ammon, Amalek and Michmash (I Samuel 11:14, 15:33). Another ritual center was situated at *Shiloh* (Joshua 18:1, 21:2; I Samuel 1:3),

THE BORDERS OF THE TRIBAL TERRITORIES

General view of Mount Tabor in Galilee (photo Samuel Magal).

where Joshua allocated the land to the seven tribes who settled to the west of the Jordan (Joshua 1). Joshua also built an altar on Mount Ebal, where he inscribed a copy of the Law of Moses (8:30–35), and at Shechem he made the covenant between the Lord and the Twelve Tribes, after which he sent each tribe to its inheritance (24:1–28). *Mount Tabor*, which was considered to be a sacred place (Psalms 89:12; Jeremiah 46:18), was also a ritual center for the tribes of Galilee. The mountain lay on the border between the four tribes of Galilee, and it was here that Deborah called upon them to war against Sisera the Canaanite (Judges 4:6, 4:12–14).

The Geographical Boundaries between the Tribes

Two types of boundary are mentioned in the Bible: *artificial*, secondary boundaries, and *natural*, primary boundaries. The artificial borders built of piles of stones and fences (Genesis 31:45–52; Job 24:2) were placed between fields and within the city (Judges 1:18; I Samuel 5:6; I Kings 18:8), or in the village enclosures (Joshua 19:8). The natural boundary, on the other hand, defined the borders of tribal lands and districts (Ezekiel 48:2–28), and delineated the borders between nations (Genesis 10:19, 47:21; Numbers 20:21, 23, 21:13, 23–24, 34:12; Deuteronomy 2:18, 3:17; Joshua 13:10, 15:21; I Samuel 11:7; I Kings 5:1).

The description of the boundaries between the Twelve Tribes in the Book of Joshua mentions 51 geographical features which include 15 types of landscape and outstanding reliefs, in addition to many settlement names, some of which were taken from names of individuals in the tribe. The geographical features include mountains, their peaks, flanks, edges and slopes; rolling country, plateaus, valleys and plains, rivers, springs, waterfalls, seas and bays, cliffs and wildernesses. Most of the features are continental with only a few mentioning marine or river features, such as springs, waterfalls, bays and seas: the Mediterranean, the Dead Sea and the Sea of Galilee. The sea constitutes the main natural boundary of the country, as we find in Jeremiah 5:22:

> which have placed the sand for the bound of the sea by a perpetual decree, that it cannot pass it:
>
> (Jeremiah 5:22)

(Other references include Numbers 34:5; Joshua 15:5, 17:10; Ezekiel 47:17, Psalms 104:9.)

The most important land boundary of the tribes is the mountain range, which is the origin of all the relief features between their lands. There are several reasons for this: firstly, *jebel* in Arabic, *gavla* in Aramaic and *geval* in Hebrew all mean mountain, and the Hebrew for border is *gvul*. Evidence of this usage is found in Psalm 78:54:

> And he brought them to the border of his sanctuary [*gvul*], even to this mountain, which his right hand had purchased.
>
> (Psalm 78:54)

where we see the parallel between the "border," or land, and "mountain," and in Joshua 13:5 where the mountain of Lebanon is termed "the land of the Giblites" (also in Psalms 108:33; Isaiah 54:12).

Secondly, most of the important tribes dwelt in the mountains on either side of the Jordan, so it was natural that the mountains and the rivers, from their source to their estuaries in the sea and the valley, should serve as main borders between the tribal territories. Out of the fifty-one features and fifteen landscapes mentioned, thirteen features

THE BORDERS OF THE TRIBES OF BENJAMIN AND ITS NEIGHBORS

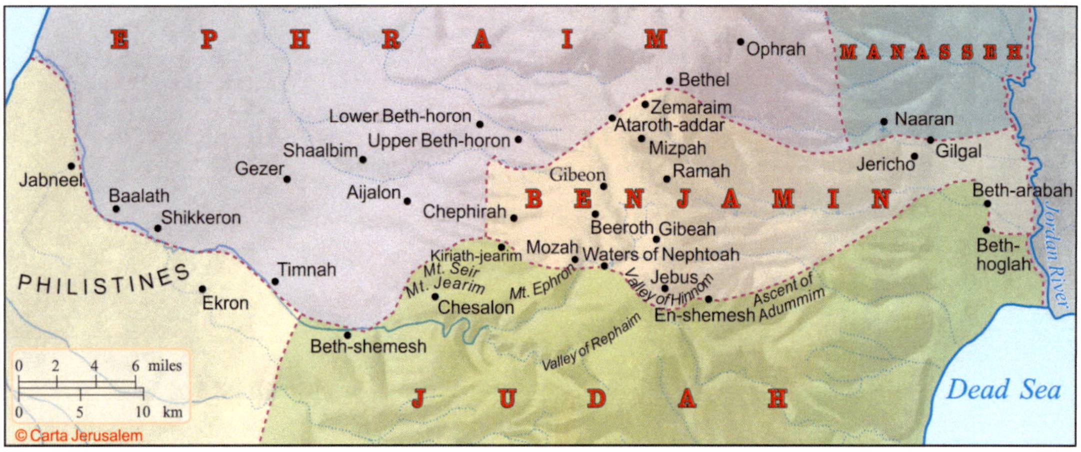

are mountains, mountaintops, peaks and plateaus, which are the watersheds and the division of routeways to the seas and valleys (Proverbs 8:2); five are mountain flanks, two are mountain slopes, so that, in all, twenty-eight features of the fifty-one are directly connected to mountains. Since the border on the mountain is not precisely defined, and since the rivers rise high in the mountains to flow to their estuaries in the seas and valleys, the river and its water sources constituted a much better-defined boundary (Numbers 22:36, 34:12; Deuteronomy 3:16–17; Joshua 12:2, 13:23, 17:9). If we add to these features the tens of rivers mentioned as tribal borders, it will become quite clear that the "mountain" and the "border" are synonymous, and constitute the main feature delineating the borders between the tribes.

In conclusion, it should be pointed out that the mountain peaks were the site of ritual centers throughout the country and in all tribal territories (Exodus 19:20; Numbers 23:14; Deuteronomy 12:2; Joshua 4:13, 8:30; I Kings 18:19–20, 19:8; I Kings 4:25; Isaiah 2:2, 11:9, 56:7, 57:13, 65:25; Ezekiel 6:13, 11:23; Psalms 68:18; II Chronicles 21:11), as stated in Micah 4:1:

> But in the last days it shall come to pass, that the mountain of the house of the LORD shall be established in the top of the mountains, and it shall be exalted above the hills; and people shall flow unto it.
>
> (Micah 4:1)

The mountains were the border between the two tribes such as Jerusalem, the mountain of Beth-el, Mount Ebal, Mizpeh-gilead and Carmel, or the border between four tribes, such as Mount Tabor on the border of Naphtali, Asher, Zebulun and Issachar. The mountains also served as lookout posts over the tribal land and other parts of the country, as described in Deuteronomy 34:1:

> Moses went up from the plains of Moab unto the mountain of Nebo, to the top of Pisgah, that is over against Jericho. And the Lord shewed him all the land, Gilead, unto Dan.
>
> (Deuteronomy 34:1)

(See also Numbers 23:9, 27:12; Deuteronomy 3:27; Song of Songs 4:8.)

The mountain, too, was also the place from which the alarm was sounded in case of war, and the battle was initiated only after the Ark of the Covenant had been brought up to the top of the mountain (Exodus 17:9–10; Numbers 14:40–44, 21:20; I Samuel 17:8; Isaiah 18:3, 30:17).

Hence we see that the mountain and the sea were the main natural boundaries of both the tribes and the Land of Israel, where the river, which rose in the mountains and flowed down to the sea or to the Jordan Valley, served as the intertribal border. The large rivers such as the Euphrates and the river of Egypt (Wadi el-Arish) also served as international boundaries, as we find in Genesis 15:18:

> In the same day the LORD made a covenant with Abram, saying, Unto thy seed have I given this land, from the river of Egypt unto the great river, the river Euphrates:
>
> (Genesis 15:18)

and in II Kings 24:7:

> And the king of Egypt came not again any more out of his land: for the king of Babylon had taken from the river of Egypt unto the river Euphrates all that pertained to the king of Egypt.
>
> (II Kings 24:7)

THE BORDERS OF THE TRIBES IN GALILEE

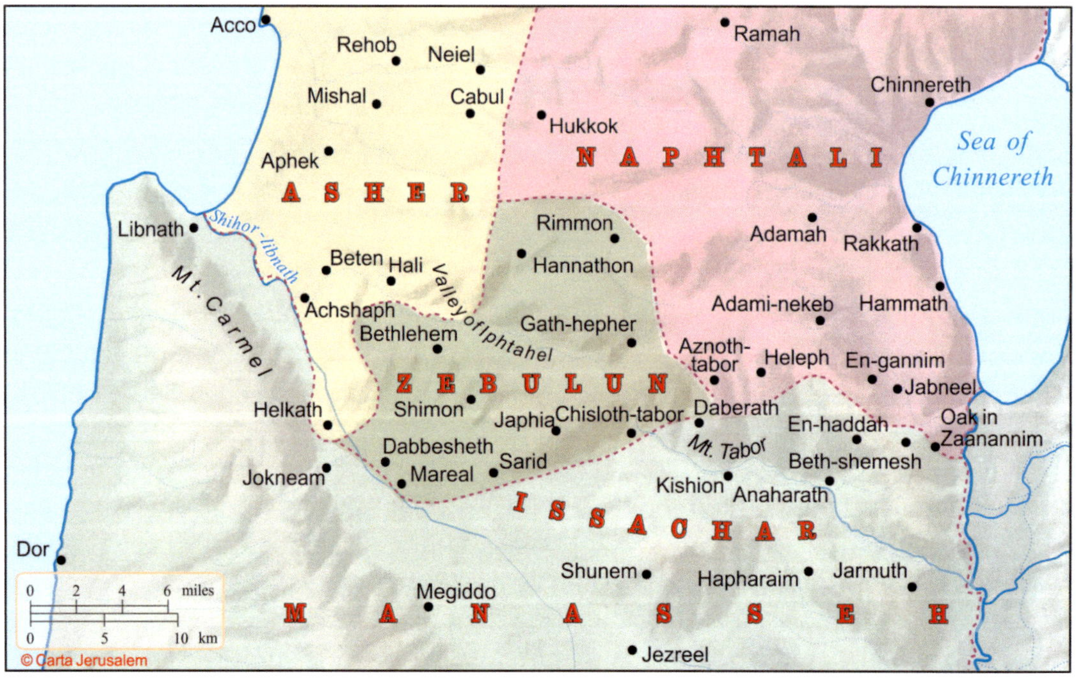

AND THERE WENT FROM THENCE...SIX HUNDRED MEN APPOINTED WITH WEAPONS OF WAR

(Judges 18:11))

In the course of our discussion of the tribe of Dan, we will locate its territory along the coast, clarify how the population obtained its weapons, the route that they used from their land to the hills of Judah and Ephraim, and the location of their places of worship along their route to Galilee.

The tribe of Judah was one of the strongest and the vanguard of the people (Numbers 2:9), whereas Dan was the rearguard:

> They shall go hindmost with their standards.
>
> (Numbers 2:31)

The Danites were in fact the second largest tribe; Judah was the largest with 74,600 soldiers, and Dan—

> And his host, and those that were numbered of them, were threescore and two thousand and seven hundred.
>
> (Numbers 2:26)

The territories of these two tribes were located on the borders of mighty enemies: Egypt, Edom, Moab and Ammon lay along the borders with Judah, while Dan was located on the borders of the Philistines, the Canaanites and the Amorites. At first, the territory of Dan extended north of the Philistines, between the Sorek Valley and its tributaries to the south the Yarkon and its tributaries in the north, adjacent to the Canaanites at Tyre, and the Amorites in the mountains to the east. To the west they were hemmed in by the Philistine coastal cities of Gath, Ekron, Tell Qasile and Aphek. Thus, they were under great pressure and were eventually pushed out of their territory (see I Samuel 7:14).

THE TRIBE OF DAN

Carts of Sea People drawn by oxen, from relief of Ramesses III at Medinet Habu.

The courage of the Danites is expressed by Moses in his blessing to the tribes of Israel in Deuteronomy 33:22, "Dan is a lion's whelp" and is also emphasized in our chapter (Judges 18) in the narrative of the *few in number* who set out to conquer new territory in Galilee:

> And there went from thence of the family of the Danites, out of Zorah and out of Eshtaol, six hundred men appointed with weapons of war.
>
> (Judges 18:11)

This is the first occasion during the period of colonization that the Bible mentions "weapons of war" solely in the possession of the Danites. This chapter refers to the Danites three times as six hundred soldiers "appointed with weapons of war." The question arises as to where they obtained these weapons, and why they are not mentioned in relation to the other tribes. Professor Y. Yadin is of the opinion that the Danites were seafaring heathens originating in the eastern Mediterranean and united with the tribe of Dan, so that the settlement of the Danites in close proximity to the Philistines along the coast, "and why did Dan remain in ships?" (Song of Deborah, Judges 5:17), caused competition between them. The Philistines were the only ironworkers in the Land of Israel (I Samuel 13:19–20), mining the ores of the Jabbok Valley and forging it in the "Valley of the Forgers" (Ge-harashim) between Lod and Ono, as mentioned in Nehemiah 11:35, in the territory of Dan. If the Danites originated in an area to the east of the iron-producing region, then they may well have taken advantage of the Philistines' iron to make their weapons of war. In their march from their territory to the hills of Ephraim and Galilee, it should be noted that they were strong enough to control the roads to the Judean Hills, as Jacob prophesied in his blessing:

> Dan shall be a serpent by the way, an adder in the path, that biteth the horse heels, so that his rider shall fall backward.
>
> (Genesis 49:17)

This passage indicates that Dan controlled the routes used

The Valley of Sorek (photo Hadas, via Wikimedia Commons).

by horse-riders, but it is not clear where these routes were. Our chapter narrates:

> And there went from thence of the family of the Danites, out of Zorah and out of Eshtaol, six hundred men appointed with weapons of war.
>
> And they went up, and pitched in Kirjathjearim, in Judah: wherefore they called that place Mahaneh-dan unto this day: behold, [it is] behind Kirjath-jearim.
>
> (Judges 18:11–12)

During the period of the Judges, the natural routeways probably followed the valleys, which had winding, snakelike courses and were the most convenient for horse-riders. Hence, it may be assumed that the Danites ascended to Kirjath-jearim via the Kesalon Valley, which rises near Kirjath-jearim and flows to its source in the Sorek Valley near Zorah and Eshtaol. The Danites also controlled the most convenient route ascending from the Shephelah to the hills of Ephraim. Evidence of Dan's control over the roads to the north of his territory, the "Sea Road" connecting the Bashan with Galilee, is found in Deuteronomy 33:22:

> And of Dan he said: Dan is a lion's whelp: he shall leap from Bashan.
>
> (Deuteronomy 33:22)

Thus the Danites probably controlled the main road climbing from the Hulah valley and Ijon which led to the kingdoms of Aram-hamath and Aram-zobah, which corresponds to the blessing given by Jacob which proclaimed that he would have a horse-riding way of life.

With regard to ritual centers we must locate the house of Micah in the hills of Ephraim, where the Levite lad served. It is interesting to note that Deborah's seat was also a ritual center. The biblical narrative states that she sat under "the Palm of Deborah," similar to the sacred terebinth of Moreh at Shechem, and the terebinths of Mamre at Hebron. Judges 4:5 relates of Deborah:

> And she dwelt under the palm tree of Deborah between Ramah and Beth-el in mount Ephraim: and the children of Israel came up to her for judgment.
>
> (Judges 4:5)

The settlement between Ramah and Beth-el was probably in the vicinity of Ramallah, where remains of the period of the Judges have been discovered at Khirbet Rathana. Further, the word *ramallah* in Arabic means "the totality of God." Hence we may assume that the city of Micah was also located in this vicinity. The five Danite spies started out from Zorah and Eshtaol:

> when they came to mount Ephraim, to the house of Micah, they lodged there.
>
> (Judges 18:2)

The distance between Zorah and Ramallah is approximately 19 miles (30 km) which could be covered in a day's walking. Thus we see that the Danites traveled from their territory on the coast to the Galilee, passing ritual centers that lay at road junctions: Eshtaol in the Shephelah, Kirjath-jearim or Kirjath-baal in Judah, Micah's city in the hills of Ephraim, and Dan in Galilee, which was the capital and ritual center of Jeroboam in the north of the Israelite kingdom.

THE MIGRATION OF THE TRIBE OF DAN

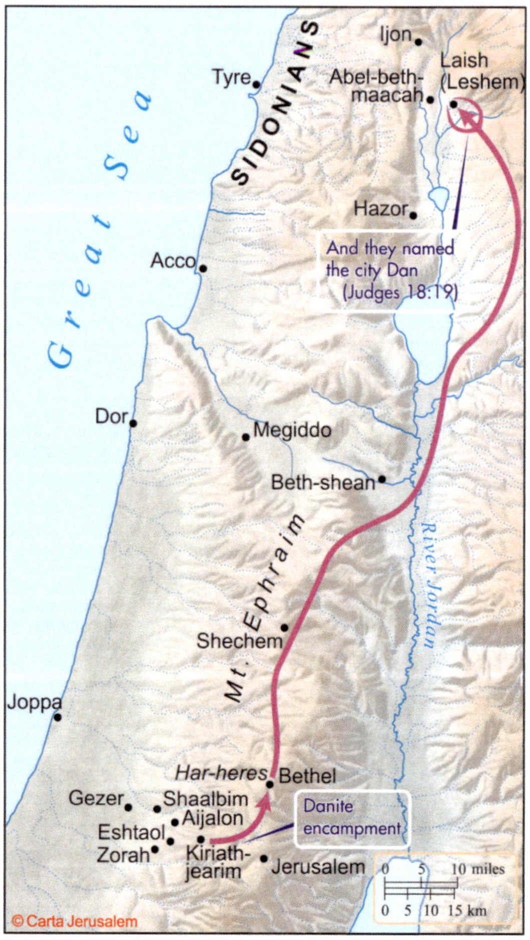

AND IT WENT OUT TO THE SOUTH SIDE TO MAALEH-ACRABBIM, AND PASSED ALONG TO ZIN, AND ASCENDED UP ON THE SOUTH SIDE UNTO KADESH-BARNEA, AND PASSED ALONG TO HEZRON, AND WENT UP TO ADAR

(Joshua 15:3)

This chapter delineates the southern border of the tribe of Judah, mentioning several locations whose identification by scholars is generally accepted, such as the "Lashon" (tongue) of the Dead Sea and Kadesh-barnea, and several others on which opinions are divided. The latter include the Ascent of Akrabbim (Scorpions), Zin, Hazar-addar and Karkaa.

The Ascent of Akrabbim is mentioned three times in the Bible. On the first occasion, Numbers 34:3–4, the southern border of the land of Canaan is delineated:

> Then your south quarter shall be from the wilderness of Zin along by the coast of Edom, and your south border shall be the outmost coast of the salt sea eastward:
>
> And your border shall turn from the south to the ascent of Akrabbim, and pass on to Zin: and the going forth thereof shall be from the south to Kadesh-barnea, and shall go on to Hazar-addar, and pass on to Azmon.
>
> (Numbers 34:3–4)

The second reference is found in the delineation of the southern border of Judah, in Joshua 15:2–3:

> And their south border was from the shore of the salt sea, from the bay that looketh southward:
>
> And it went out to the south side to Maaleh-acrabbim, and passed along to Zin, and ascended up on the south side unto Kadesh-barnea, and passed along to Hezron, and went up to Adar, and fetched a compass to Karkaa:
>
> (Joshua 15:2–3)

On the third occasion, Judges 1:36 describes the Amorite border:

> And the coast of the Amorites was from the going up to Akrabbim, from the rock and upward.
>
> (Judges 1:36)

Some scholars locate the Ascent of Akrabbim with the present road of the same name, to the southwest of the Dead Sea, while Sela is identified with Petra since the Greek word *petra* means a rock, and *sela* in Hebrew is also a rock. Professor B. Mazar, however, claims that the biblical Ascent of Akrabbim lies to the east of the Jordan, at a place known today as Umm el Aqareb, meaning "scorpion's mother." This view is based on the fact that Numbers 34 delineates the border, "the outmost coast of the salt sea eastward." Professor Mazar locates Zin and Sela in the villages of Danna and Sila, high up in the northern Edomite mountains near Buseira, which is probably identical to biblical Bozrah. This hypothesis is based on the interchange of the letters "d" and "z" in Hebrew and Arabic (the Hebrew Zin becoming Arabic Danna, whereas Sela and Sila retain the same constant "s"). These two settlements lay on the biblical King's Highway, guarding the copper mines in the biblical Ge-harashim, located in Wadi Nehas.

At this site N. Glueck discovered remains of copper mines dating from the time of the Kenites and the kingdom of Judah. Sela was in fact the Kenite capital; the Kenites were

IT WENT OUT TO THE SOUTH SIDE TO MAALEH-ACRABBIM (JOSHUA 15:3)

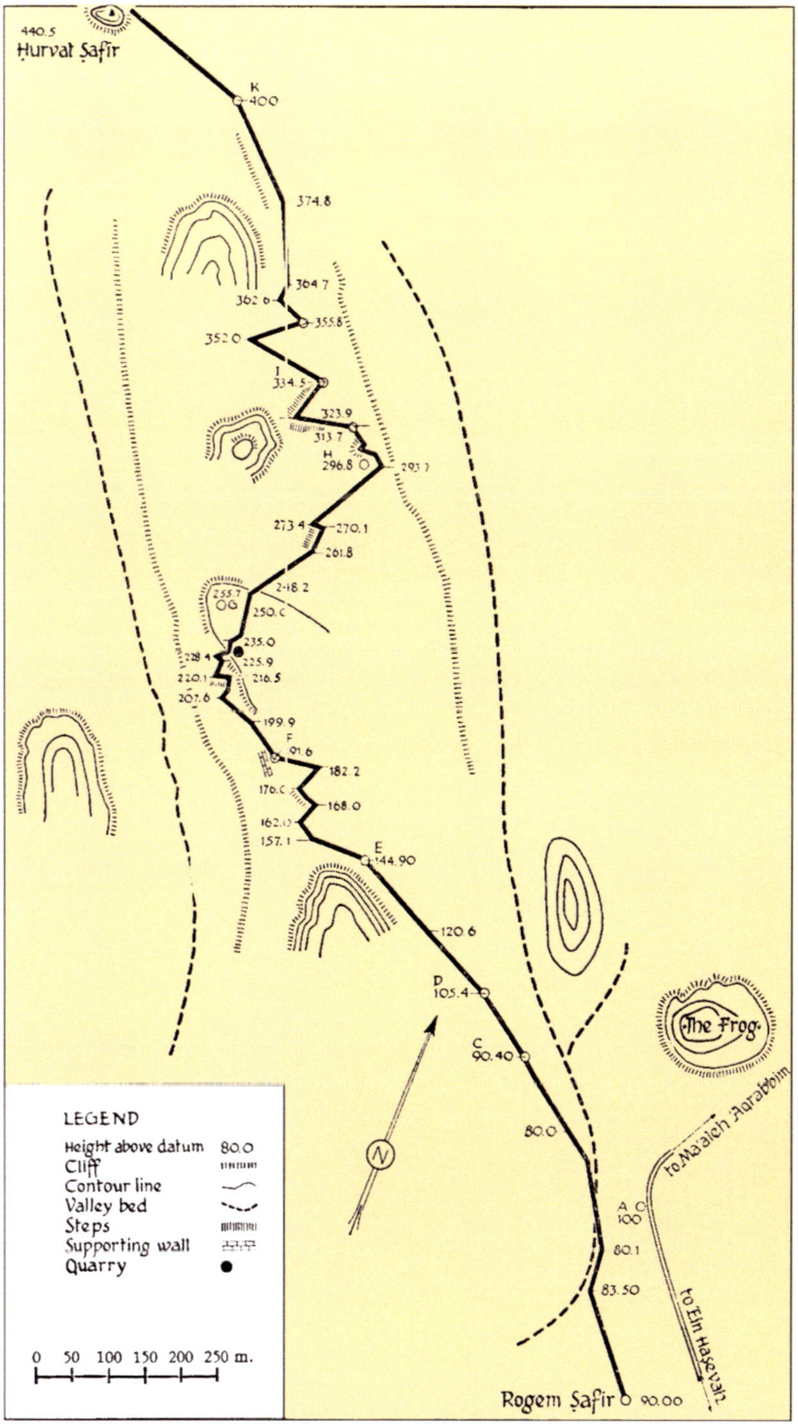

coppersmiths of the tribe of Judah, as we find in Balaam's parable:

> And he looked on the Kenites, and took up his parable, and said, Strong is thy dwellingplace, and thou puttest thy nest in a rock [*sela*].
>
> (Numbers 24:21)

Thus it was natural that the southern border of Judah should include the copper mines which were important to the economy, and should control the trade route which followed the "King's Road" from Elath to the north.

The Book of Joshua mentions two locations, Hezron and Addar, while the Book of Numbers mentions only Hazar-addar. Similarly, Karkaa is mentioned only in Joshua, and not in Numbers. We feel that the two names, Hazar-addar and Karkaa, refer to one and the same place—the round crater of Gebel el-Maghara, southwest of Kadesh-barnea on the way to the Mediterranean Sea, for the following reasons. Firstly, many craters in the Negeb and Sinai are termed by the Arabs *hadira*, which is written in Arabic with the sound "z" like Hazera. The meaning of this term is a permanent settlement, in contrast to other parts of the wilderness which are inhabited by nomads. Most of the craters have both cultivated land and water supplies. Thus the round crater of Gebel el-Maghara, which is bounded by rocky walls making it a fenced area, gives the name *hazer* (in Hebrew, courtyard), "Hezron" and "Hazeroth," which in the Bible are synonymous with craters. Within the crater of Maghara we find springs and wells.

The second part of the place name "addar" may be compared with the Aramaic *idar* mentioned in Daniel 2:35 and in *Bereshit Rabba* 63, which means a barn, or threshing floor. It has been used in the borrowed sense of a round place of assembly. We see, then, that not only does the crater of Maghara possess large areas of fertile soil, which are cultivated by the Bedouin to this day, but they are the only croplands in the sand dunes of this desert region, and may thus be correlated to the "Karkaa" (Hebrew *qarqa'a* = soil) which is mentioned only once in the whole of the Bible.

Lion (Frog) Rock in Ma'aleh Aqrabbim (Dr. Avishai Teicher Pikiwiki Israel, via Wikimedia Commons).

THE RIVER OF EGYPT

Scholars are divided in their opinion as to the lcoation of the Wadi of Egypt. Some claim that it may be identified with Wadi el-Arish, whereas others hold that it refers to the Pelusium near Tell el-Farama to the west of the Sirbonnic Sea. Before giving our opinion on the subject, let us examine the biblical references to "river" [*nahar*] and "the wadi [*nahal*] of Egypt." Genesis 15:18 states:

> In the same day the LORD made a covenant with Abram, saying, Unto thy seed have I given this land, from the river of Egypt unto the great river, the river Euphrates:
>
> (Genesis 15:18)

This passage delineates the southwestern boundary of the country as the river of Egypt. Numbers 34:4–5 mentions the river of Egypt again as a boundary:

> And your border shall turn from the south to the ascent of Akrabbim, and pass on to Zin: and the going forth thereof shall be from the south to Kadeshbarnea, and shall go on to Hazaraddar, and pass on to Azmon:
>
> And the border shall fetch a compass from Azmon unto the river of Egypt, and the goings out of it shall be at the sea.
>
> (Numbers 34:4–5)

There are several other biblical sources in this vein. Thus we see that the southwestern boundary of the Land of Israel is delineated once as the river of Egypt and once as the Wadi of Egypt. The Aramaic translation of the Wadi of Egypt in Numbers 34:5 is explained by the interpreter, Jonathan, as follows:

> the boundary passed from Kesam (Azmon) to the Nile of Egypt.

Similar explanations are found in the Jerusalem Talmud, in Rashi and in Radak.

In our opinion it is important to differentiate between the Wadi of Egypt mentioned here, which refers to the eastern and smallest arm of the Nile, and the *river of Egypt*, which refers to the main tributary valley of the Egyptian Nile. The Egyptian word *shihor* means the river of the Egyptian god Horus. At the delta the Nile divides into seven distributaries, as we find in Isaiah 11:15:

> The LORD shall utterly destroy the tongue of the Egyptian sea; and with his mighty wind shall he shake his hand over the river and shall smite it in the seven streams, and make men go over dryshod. (Isaiah 11:15)

Only two of these seven distributaries are large: the Rosetta to the east of Alexandria and Damietta to the west of Port Said, which is probably the Nile or Shihor of Egypt.

The Greek, Roman and Byzantine maps of Ptolemy, Madaba, Peutinger and others, as well as recent research show that before the construction of the Suez Canal one

(I Kings 8:65)

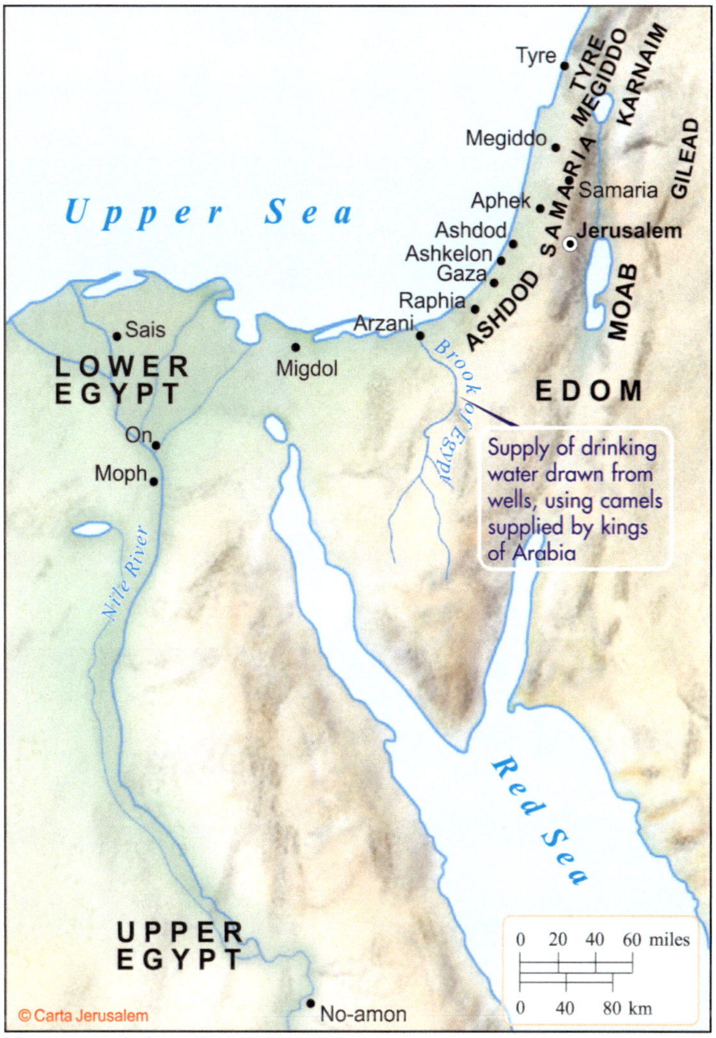

THE BROOK OF EGYPT

of the arms of the Nile—the Pelusium—used to flow in a northeasterly direction into the west of the Sirbonnic Sea, where the port of Pelusium was built. This port is designated on the above maps, and has been identified at Tell el-Farama near the military camp of Balluza. This was apparently the border which ran from Kadesh-barnea to the river of Egypt and the Mediterranean Sea. It was named the river of Egypt since it originated in Egypt, whereas Wadi el-Arish, held by some scholars to be the river of Egypt, rises in the Sinai peninsula and the Negeb and *not* in Egypt, and has therefore no connection whatsoever with Egypt. Similarly the rivers of Assyria, Babylon, Damascus and the Jordan all flow in their respective countries, as described in Genesis 2:14:

> The name of the third river is Hiddekel: that is it which goeth toward the east of Assyria. And the fourth river is the Euphrates. (Genesis 2:14)

Psalm 137:1 also mentions rivers:

> By the rivers of Babylon, there we sat down, yea, we wept, when we remembered Zion. (Psalm 137:1)

II Kings 5:12 describes the rivers of Damascus:

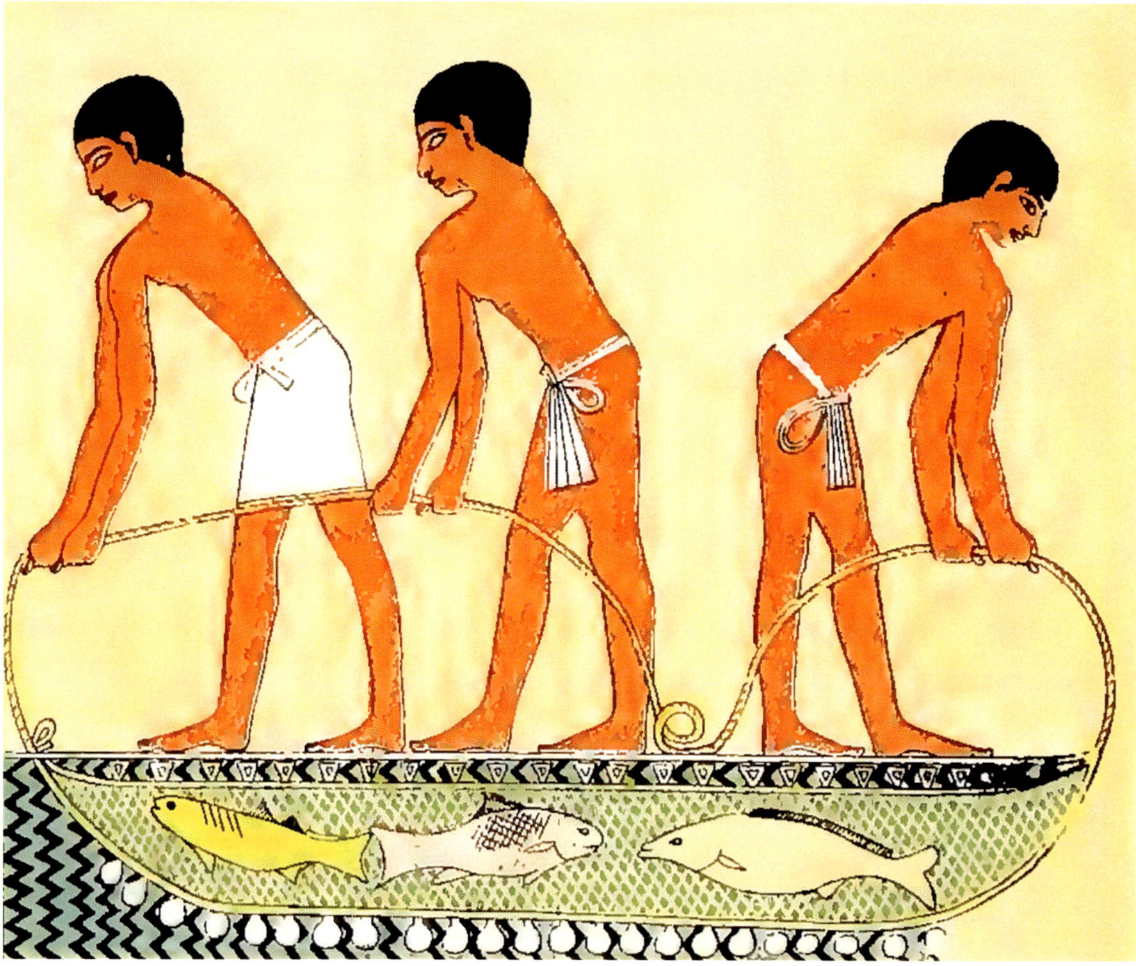

Fishermen, from a section of the painted wall in the tomb of Ra-hotep at Medum (Petrie 1892, pl. 10).

> Are not Abanah and Pharpar, rivers of Damascus, better than all the waters of Israel?
>
> II Kings 5:12)

The Jordan is mentioned in Ezekiel 47:18:

> ...and from Gilead, and from the land of Israel by Jordan, from the border unto the eas sea....
>
> (Ezekiel 47:18)

So it is reasonable to assume that the Wadi of Egypt was, in fact, the Pelusium, which was the easternmost and smallest branch of the Nile, and which is now dry, while the river of Egypt is one of the main Nile distributaries, flowing out into the sea to the west of Port Said, at the city of Damietta. Wadi el-Arish cannot, in our opinion, be identified with the river of Egypt, firstly because of its distance from Egypt, and secondly because its shallow waters at the estuary limit its ability to serve as a well-defined boundary. Furthermore, it is often a dry wadi, subject to flooding—according to recent studies, only every three years. The rivers of Egypt we have described, however, are permanent streams with an abundant flow, since Egypt is well-known as a country of irrigated crops.

The source of this error is interesting. It originated in the Septuagint translation of the Bible, which was copied by the Christian bishop Eusebius, who stated that the Wadi of Egypt mentioned in Isaiah 72:12 was Rinocorura, identified today with El-Arish. The Christian scholar Hieronymus (St. Jerome) pointed out this mistake, explaining that this name (Rinocorura) is a Septuagint addition, not found in the Hebrew original.

In the light of all these facts, we may assume that the Wadi of Egypt mentioned in the Bible as the border of the Land of Israel lies in the small, eastern Pelusian branch of the Nile, as mentioned in I Kings 8:65:

> And at that time Solomon held a feast, and all Israel with him, a great congregation, from the entering in of Hamath unto the river of Egypt, before the LORD our God, seven days.
>
> (I Kings 8:65)

Satellite view of the River Nile (NASA; photo Jacques Descloitres, MODIS Land Science Team)

THE SONS OF SIMEON...WENT TO MOUNT SEIR

(I Chronicles 4:42)

This chapter relates a strange incident regarding the tribe of Simeon:

> And some of them, even of the sons of Simeon, five hundred men, went to mount Seir, having for their captains Pelatiah, and Neariah, and Rephaiah, and Uzziel, the sons of Ishi.
>
> And they smote the rest of the Amalekites that were escaped, and dwelt there unto this day.
>
> (I Chronicles 4:42–43)

Before discussing this strange event of the invasion of Mount Seir by a small number of Simeonites, it is important to clarify the limits of Amalekite expansion in the Negeb, the territory of the tribe of Simeon, and finally the location of Mount Seir. The Amalekites, who were early desert caravan leaders, settled in the Negeb during the time of the Patriarchs, who fought against their four kings of Shinar at Kadesh. They are also found in this region during the period of the Israelites' wanderings in the wildernesses of Sinai. The Amalekites expanded throughout the Negeb, as mentioned in Numbers 13:29:

> Amalekites dwell in the land of the south;

with their base at Kadesh-barnea, the best-watered oasis in the whole of the Negeb and northern Sinai (Genesis 14:7). The Amalekites probably originated in the mountains of Edom, through which the biblical King's Highway or the Spice Route from Arabia passed, and their aim in locating themselves *in the four corners of the Negeb* was to gain control over the main transportation routes of the whole region. Their control over the southeastern Negeb on the border of Edom, and the southwest on the Egyptian border, is mentioned in the narrative of Saul's war against the Amalekites in I Samuel 15:7:

> Saul smote the Amalekites, from Havilah until thou comest to Shur, that is over against Egypt.
>
> (I Samuel 15:7; see also I Samuel 27:8)

From this campaign it emerges that the Amalekites controlled the Arabah road in the east that leads to Ezion-geber, the export and import outlet on the Red Sea, as well as the southern tip of the King's Highway. In the west they were positioned on the Way of Shur, leading from Beersheba to the Egyptian border as far as Klysma, the Egyptian Red Sea port, and the southern tip of the "Via Maris." In the northwestern Negeb the Amalekites of David's time reached as far as Ziklag, along the Besor River which flowed into the Mediterranean at Gaza, the southern port of the Philistines (I Samuel 30:1, 30:10–14). The Amalekites apparently penetrated the northeastern Negeb via the Arabah, and it was in the city of Amalek in the territory of the Kenite Negeb that Saul struck the Amalekites in their attempted retreat via the Arabah to Havilah in Edom (I Samuel 15:5–7). The desert-dwelling

THE KINGS OF THE NORTH (GENESIS 14)

A camel caravan in the desert (photo Yoavd, via Wikimedia Commons).

Amalekites probably gained control over the Negeb because of their success in training their camels for war:

> David smote them from the twilight even unto the evening of the next day: and there escaped not a man of them, save four hundred young men, which rode upon camels and fled.
>
> (I Samuel 30:17)

This passage in I Samuel 30:17 describes David's campaign against the Amalekites in the Besor Valley, which teaches us of the existence of the first camel-borne armed force in the Bible.

The tribe of Simeon dwelling in the Judean Negeb lived to the west of Judah, from Sharuhen in the Besor Valley in the west as far as Beer-sheba in the east. It may be assumed that the Simeonites were in control of the Way of Shur, which led from Beer-sheba in their territory along the Besor, Nizzana and El-Arish valleys to Kadesh-barnea, the center of the Amalekites. Hence Simeon was very close to Amalekite territory. We learn of the courage displayed by Simeon and his family in the story of Dinah, when he and Levi, his shepherd brother, smote every male and the chief of the Hivites in Shechem, which was inhabited, alien territory (Genesis 34:2, 34:25–26). It was no coincidence that Joseph took Simeon as hostage when his brothers came to buy food in Egypt (Genesis 42:24, 43:23). Simeon was the third largest of the tribes of Israel, with 59,300 soldiers, compared with 74,600 in Judah and 62,700 in Dan (Numbers 1:22–23, 1:26–27, 1:39). It would appear that the Simeonites were under greater pressure from the Amalekites than the Negeb Calebites, the Jerahmeelites and the Kenites, since the Amalekites penetrated westward as far as the Philistine border even before the Philistines settled on the coast, later to curb their progress when they carried out their invasions as far as Gaza (I Samuel 8:12; I Chronicles 18:11; I Samuel 27:8; Judges 6:4).

With regard to the invasion of Mount Seir by the Simeonites, we should emphasize that Simeon never dwelt in Edom. Hence Mount Seir mentioned here must be located at Gebel esh-Sha'ira to the northwest of Elath (Grid Ref. 009.888). This mountain rises to 3,380 feet (1,030 m) above sea level, and its name in Arabic means "goat's hair." It also constitutes the watershed of three rivers and transport axes: northwest—Wadi el-Arish; northeast—the Paran River; and south—the Watir Valley that penetrates eastern Sinai. Supporting evidence may be found in the location of Gebel Zoob Shamoun (Grid Ref. 096.924), at 2,220 feet (677 m), since *zoob* in Arabic means hairy, and the reference to Simeon, which has no significance semantically in Arabic, hints at the settlement of this tribe with its flocks at this important junction. Thus the brave descendants of Simeon managed to push out the last of the Amalekites remaining in the Negeb after their defeat by Saul and David. It may by assumed, albeit only as a hypothesis, that the Simeonites only managed to drive the Amalekites out after they themselves had trained camels and established a camel-borne force. It would have been impossible for them to gain advantage over the camel-riding desert highwaymen without the use of the same beast of war.

THY FATHER WAS AN AMORITE

(Ezekiel 16:3)

This chapter deals with the Amorites in Jerusalem, and discusses their origins, where they settled in Canaan, their occupations, their ritual, and the location of the "Way of the Mountain of the Amorites" in the Negeb.

The Amorites are mentioned in Accadian documents from as far back as the third millennium BCE until the first millennium, under the name Amuru, which means west in the Accadian language. The kings of Accad obtained stone and marble for building from the Amuru. From the fifteenth century BCE the Egyptians ruled the Amuru, and this fact is mentioned in the El-Amarna tablets and Hittite documents, where their kingdom is said to lie in middle and lower Syria. Tur-Sinai attributes the word Amorite to the root *amir* or *amor*, meaning high or uplifted. The Amorites, who were western Semitic people, did in fact dwell in the forested regions of Mount Lebanon, as described in the Book of Joshua:

> From the south, all the land of the Canaanites, and Mearah that is beside the Sidonians, unto Aphek, to the borders of the Amorites.
>
> (Joshua 13:4)

Aphek is situated in Lebanon to the east of Gebal. Amos, too, suggests that the Amorites originated in the forested mountains of Lebanon:

> Yet destroyed I the Amorite before them, whose height was like the height of the cedars and he was as strong as the oaks.
>
> (Amos 2:9)

The Amorite origins in Syria in proximity to the Hittites resulted in their being mentioned in conjunction with one another on numerous occasions in the Bible. Numbers 13:29 tells us of the precise geographical location of the nations of Canaan:

> The Amalekites dwell in the land of the south: and the Hittites, and the Jebusites, and the Amorites, dwell in the mountains: and the Canaanites dwell by the sea, and by the coast of Jordan.
>
> (Numbers 13:29)

During the period of colonization, the Amalekites settled in the Negeb, the Canaanites settled in the plains, valleys and the Jordan depression which were topographically convenient, and are mentioned 154 times in the Bible, more so than any other nation, while the Amorites who originated in the mountains settled in the rocky hill country on either side of the Jordan, and are mentioned 86 times in the Bible. Hence two expressions are common in the Bible: "the land of the Amorites," and "the mountain of the Amorites." The land of the Amorites is mentioned six times in the Bible (Numbers 21:31; Joshua 24:8; Judges 10:8, 11:21; Amos 2:10; Nehemiah 9:8), where four references relate to the eastern side of the Jordan, one to part of the mountains of Israel, and one to the whole of the hill country of Israel. Thus we see that the extended borders of Canaan included all of Israel, while the more limited territory included only the coastal plain, the valleys and the Jordan depression, without the central and southern Negeb. The land and mountain of the Amorites, however, lay on either side of the Jordan, including Moab, Gilead and Bashan in the east, with their chief cities of Heshbon in the kingdom of Sihon and Ashtaroth in the Bashan, as well as the mountains of Samaria, Judah and the Negeb to the west of the Jordan, with their chief cities of Hebron and Jerusalem in Judah, and Shechem in Samaria. After the Amorites were driven out of the country by the Israelites, the mountain of the Amorite is termed "the mountain of Israel" fifteen times in the Bible.

The original occupation of the mountain-dwelling Amorites, who lived in the rocky forested regions on the border of the wilderness, was probably livestock rearing. Their territory was uninterrupted on the eastern side of the Jordan, from Moab and Gilead to the Bashan—the finest breeding grounds for flocks in the whole of Israel. The word *imar* in Aramaic—a language which developed from the tongue of the Amorites–mentioned in Ezra 6:9, 6:17 and 7:17, means a lamb or sheep. Hence we may assume that the Amorites' chief occupation was the rearing of sheep and cattle.

Caravan of Asiatics, tomb wall painting at Beni Hassan, 1890 BCE.

ANCIENT ROUTES IN THE HOLY LAND

With regard to the ritual practices of the Amorites, their altars and temples were obviously located in fertile regions on mountaintops, under the green trees of the forest, in valleys and near the flowing water sources in the mountains. The most important gods of the Amorites included the fertility gods symbolizing vegetation, woman and abundant flocks. These idols were *hamanim*, which is expounded in the Septuagint version of Leviticus 26:30 as artifacts made of wood, and *asherah* made out of an uprooted tree in the shape of a tombstone (Deuteronomy 16:21–22), worshiped in Samaria, Beth-el and Jerusalem. The prophet Isaiah prophesies the overthrow of these peoples and their idols:

> And he shall not look to the altars, the work of his hands, neither shall respect that which his fingers have made, either the groves, or the images [*hamanim*].
>
> In that day shall his strong cities be as a forsaken bough, and an uppermost branch, which they left because of the children of Israel: and there shall be desolation.
>
> (Isaiah 17:8–9)

The Septuagint renders the "Hivites and the Amorites deserted" as the abandonment of the Land of Israel by the Hivites and the Amorites. Ezekiel prophesies against the idolatrous practices of Israelites who worshiped the Amorite gods:

> And say, Ye mountains of Israel, hear the word of the Lord GOD; Thus saith the Lord GOD to the mountains, and to the hills, to the rivers, and to the valleys; Behold, I, even I, will bring a sword upon you, and I will destroy your high places.
>
> And your altars shall be desolate, and your images shall be broken: and I will cast down your slain men before your idols.
>
> (Ezekiel 6:3–4; see also Joshua 24:15; Judges 6:10)

The Amorites had other idols including Ashtaroth, the Canaanite goddess of fertility, who gave her name to their capital in Bashan (Deuteronomy 1:4), and Chemosh, the god of war in the Moabite and Ammonite pantheon. It should be noted that in the Mesha Stone, line 17, there is some confusion between Chemosh and Ashtar, which in the Hebrew *Biblical Encyclopedia*, under Ashtorah, is explained as the planet Venus.

The Way of the Mountain of the Amorites is mentioned in the wanderings of the Israelites in the wilderness:

> And when we departed from Horeb, we went through all that great and terrible wilderness, which ye saw by the way of the mountain of the Amorites, as the LORD our God commanded us; and we came to Kadeshbarnea. 20 And I said unto you, Ye are come unto the mountain of the Amorites, which the LORD our God doth give unto us
>
> (Deuteronomy 1:19–20)

Where, then, is the mountain of the Amorites in the Negeb, and the Way of the Mountain of the Amorites? Since Deuteronomy 1:2 states that:

The Mesha Stone from Dibon (NEAEHL).

> (There are eleven days journey from Horeb by the way of mount Seir, to Kadesh-barnea.)
>
> (Deuteronomy 1:2)

the mountain of the Amorites must lie between Seir and Kadesh-barnea. Mount Seir has been identified with Gebel esh-Sha'ira to the south of Kadesh-barnea. The highest mountain between Mount Seir and Kadesh-barnea is Har (Mount) Saggi, which rises to an altitude of 3,330 feet (1,015 m) above sea level, and which is known in Arabic as Gebel Sammawa, meaning the mountain of heaven. This mountain could be the mountain of the Amorites, both in view of the meaning of *amir* and *amor* as high, or uplifted, and also because of the Arabic connotation which suggests a ritual site. The Way of the Mountain of the Amorites probably ran along Darb el-Ghazza, leading northward from Gebel esh-Sha'ira via Kuntillet 'Ajrud (Hurbat Teman), where Z. Meshel found an Israelite fortress and shrine, and west of Har Saggi on the way to Kadesh-barnea.

SIN, THE STRENGTH OF EGYPT

(Ezekiel 30:15)

The verse quoted here declares:

> I will pour my fury upon Sin, the strength of Egypt,
>
> (Ezekiel 30:15)

and raises three questions: the location of Sin; why it is termed "the stronghold of Egypt," and what was the occupation of the inhabitants of Sin in biblical times and during the Second Temple period.

Most scholars are unanimous in their view that Sin is identical to the port of Pelusium, which was discovered at Tell el-Farama on the Mediterranean coast, east of the modern Suez Canal near the military camp of Balluza in northern Sinai. This port was founded at the estuary of the easterly branch of the Nile, which formerly drained into the Mediterranean at this spot but was cut off during the period of Muslim rule in the eighth century CE. According to the geologist T. Weissbrod and the archaeologist A. Goren, Sin is mentioned as a port in the writings of Josephus and in the external non-Jewish sources, under the name of Pelusium. As to its connotation as "the stronghold of Egypt," it should be emphasized that Sin was the only port in northeastern Egypt, and lay on the border between Africa and Asia. Since this port was situated on the estuary of the Nile, surrounded by lakes and shallow marshes which prevented overland passage and acted as a barrier for shipping, Sin served as a continental and coastal border fortress on the ancient Via Maris. Thus Ezekiel terms it "the strength of Egypt."

Contemporary, 7th century statue of Egyptian pharaoh Psammetichus (Psamtik) from the Hieropolis Archeology Museum in Pamukkale, Turkey. Statue was originally found in Kale. The inscription is written in Ionian Greek and reads, "Pedon son of Amphimeos set me up as a votive, having brought [me] back from Egypt; and to him Psammetichos, king of Egypt, gave as prizes a golden armlet and a city on account of his valor." (photo Bantosh, via Wikimedia Commons)

EGYPT OF THE EXODUS

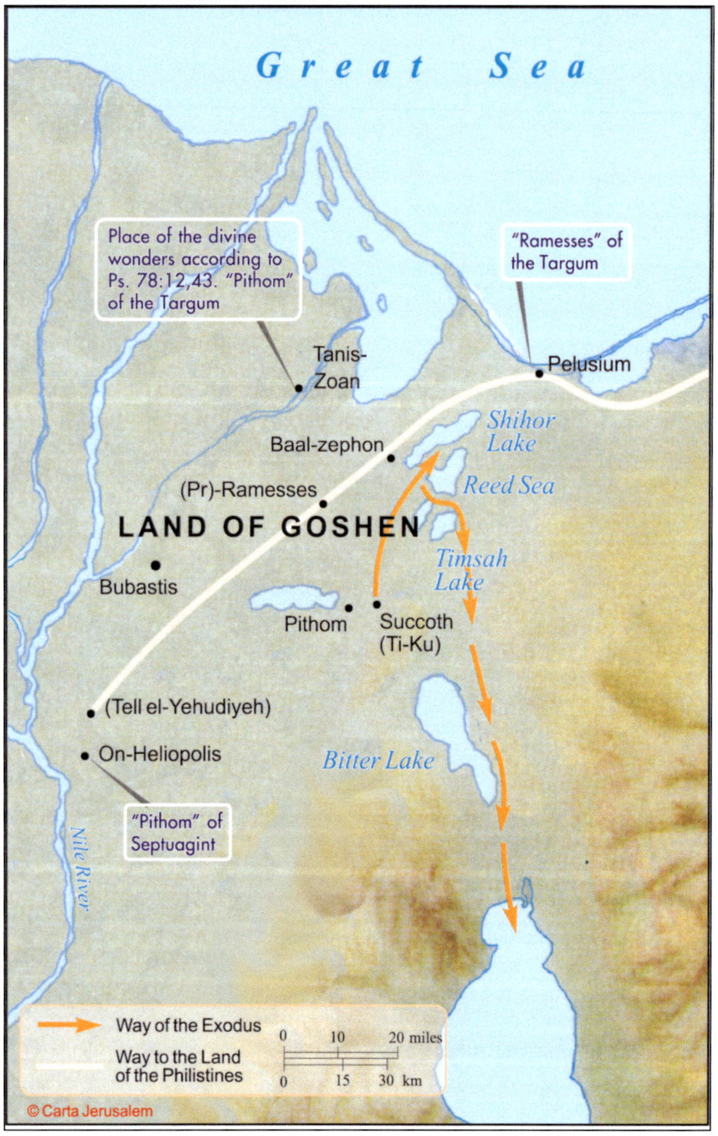

Sin's importance increased during the period of alien rule in Egypt, when foreign mercenaries were stationed there in the eighth century BCE. We learn of the flight of the Jews and their army officers to Egypt during the time of Psammetichus, the Egyptian foreign ruler, after the destruction of the First Temple by the Babylonians, in II Kings 25:26:

> And all the people, both small and great, and the captains of the armies, arose, and came to Egypt: for they were afraid of the Chaldees.
>
> (II Kings 25:26)

Jeremiah also relates that the army officers under Johanan son of Kareah and Azariah son of Hoshaiah, with the refugees from Judah, went to Egypt (ch. 43). These Jews apparently established a Hebrew army colony in Sin, the northern stronghold of Egypt, as they did at Elephantine on the southern border of Egypt, according to the papyri discovered at the fortress there. This Hebrew military colony is mentioned in the letters of Aristotle 12–13, which state that during the rule of Psammetichus in the seventh century BCE, in the period of Persian rule over Egypt in the sixth century and during the reign of Ptolemy in the fourth century, the Hebrew army was stationed in Egypt:

> At that time he [Ptolemy] transported approximately ten

thousand people from the land of the Jews to Egypt. Three thousand were young armed men and he settled them in Egypt. Before this, many Jews had come there with the king of Persia. Even earlier, others had been sent to help Psammetichus in his campaign against the king of the Ethiopians.

The inhabitants of Sin had varied occupations: they were employed in commercial activities, fishing, agriculture and industry. Sin, or Pelusium, was important commercially not only because it was situated on the Via Maris on the border of Egypt, but also because it lay about 90 miles (150 km) north of the Gulf of Suez, and the chief trade route of the Middle East passed via the Gulf of Suez and Klysma. The ancient "Suez Canal" was constructed by Pharaoh Neco in the seventh century BCE from the Gulf of Suez to the Mediterranean, and was renovated by Darius in the sixth century, as shown in reliefs made along the ancient route. Fishing at Pelusium was also varied, with fish caught in the open sea, in the lakes and salt marshes, as well as in the Nile, which was brimming with marine life. Reference to the choice fish is made in the Talmud in the time of Rabbi Abbahu, head of the Yeshiva of Caesarea in the fourth century CE.

> Rabbi Abbahu announced in Caesarea that fish entrails and fish roe may be purchased from anybody, since the presumption is that they only come from Pelusium and Aspamia.
>
> (*Avodah Zara* 39a)

The island of Elephantine, where papyri were found.

The fertile alluvial soils of the Nile valley were suitable for the cultivation of choice flax called pelusion, hence the term "louse" for shirts in Arabic and in many European languages, and the name "Balluza" given to the nearby camp. The fine-quality linen material was exported throughout the world, and is mentioned in the tractate of the Mishnah, *Yoma*, which deals with the garments worn by the High Priest on the Day of Atonement:

> In the morning he used to put on Pelusian linen worth twelve maneh and in the afternoon Indian linen.
>
> (*Yoma* 3,7)

The inhabitants also dyed the flax purple, as assumed by the piles of snail shells discovered at Tell el-Farama. Ezekiel 30:6 also mentioned a southern fort in Egypt manned by Jewish forces, on the island of Syene or modern Aswan:

> Thus saith the LORD; They also that uphold Egypt shall fall; and the pride of her power shall come down: from the tower of Syene.
>
> (Ezekiel 30:6)

There is also an assumption that the northern fortress of Egypt was called Migdol in the time of Jeremiah, who states in verse 44:1:

> The word that came to Jeremiah concerning all the Jews which dwell in the land of Egypt, which dwell at Migdol, and at Tahpanhes, and at Noph, and in the country of Pathros.
>
> (Jeremiah 40:1)

Thus we can safely assume that mercenary Hebrew forces were stationed in Egypt at two fortresses: Migdol–Sin on the northern border, and Syene–Elephantine in the far south.

FROM THE LAND OF SINIM

(Isaiah 49:12)

The full quotation of the prophet here runs as follows:

> Behold, these shall come from far: and, lo, these from the north and from the west; and these from the land of Sinim.
>
> (Isaiah 49:12)

The meaning of this passage is that God will gather in the exiles of Israel from the four corners of the earth and bring them back to Zion. Three directions are mentioned without any identification of the countries concerned, while the fourth is mentioned by name—the land of Sinnim. Three questions arise here: the location of the land of Sinnim, the activities of the exiles of Israel in this land, and the meaning of the name "Sinnim."

The location of the land of Sinnim should be sought in the south. Rashi and Jonathan interpret it "from a southern land," while the commentaries of Radak and Mezudat David also state: "it is the southern corner." Modern scholars identify Sinnim with Syene near modern Aswan on the southern Egyptian border of Sudan. Evidence is found in Ezekiel 29:10, whose prophecy runs:

> ...and I will make the land of Egypt utterly waste and desolate, from the tower of Syene even unto the border of Ethiopia.
>
> (Ezekiel 29:10)

When, then, did the Jews reach this remote region and what did they do there? The generally accepted theory is that Jews began to settle in Egypt when foreign rulers controlled the country. After the Assyrians captured Samaria at the beginning of the eighth century BCE, they resettled the Jewish and other refugees as mercenaries on the Egyptian border to defend themselves against the Ethiopic dynasty. These Jewish refugees remained in Egypt even after the Assyrians were defeated by Psammetichus in 650 BCE. The Bible relates something of the flight of the Jews and their army officers to Egypt during the time of the destruction of Jerusalem by the king of Babylon:

> And all the people, both small and great, and the captains of the armies, arose, and came to Egypt: for they were afraid of the Chaldees.
>
> (II Kings 25:26)

Jeremiah also mentions that the army officers under Johanan son of Kareah and Azariah son of Hoshaiah went down to Egypt with the Judean refugees, and their places of residence in Egypt are mentioned in verse 44:1:

> The word that came to Jeremiah concerning all the Jews which dwell in the land of Egypt, which dwell at Migdol, and at

THE EXILE FROM JUDAH AND THE FLIGHT TO EGYPT

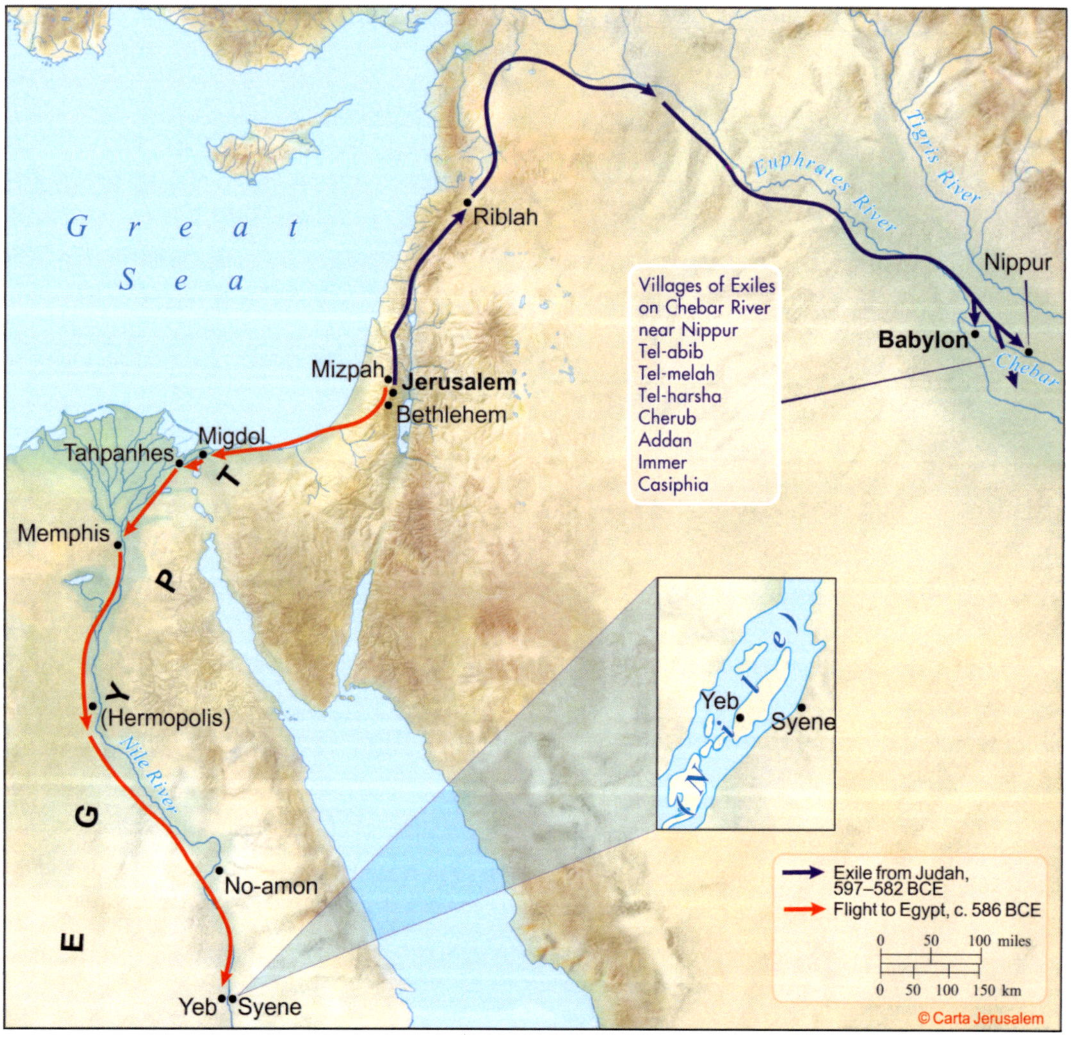

A felucca sailing through the Nile near Aswan, Egypt; in the background is the island of Elephantine (photo Przemyslaw "Blueshade" Idzkiewicz, via Wikimedia Commons).

Tahpanhes, and at Noph, and in the country of Pathros....

(Jeremiah 44:1)

The cities in order of their geographical location are, then, as follows: Migdol in the north, followed by Tahpanhes which was Daphnae; Noph, which was Memphis near Cairo; and finally the land of Pathros in Upper Egypt, in the south. When Egypt was ruled by foreigners, such as the Nubians, the Libyans, the Ethiopians, the Assyrians, the Persians and the Hellenists, foreign mercenary soldiers were stationed at these forts. Hence military and civilian Jewish settlements were founded on the borders of Egypt during the time of the Assyrian monarchy, when an alliance was made between Judah and Egypt, during the time of the destruction of Jerusalem by the Babylonians, as well as in the Persian period and more particularly in the Ptolemaic era. In Cleopatra's time, Hebrew officers led her army, and during the time of Onias a central Jewish sanctuary was built in Egypt.

We will now discuss the occupation of the inhabitants of the land of Sinnim on the southern border of Egypt. At the end of the nineteenth century, papyri were found at Elephantine, so named because of the ivory brought there from Ethiopia. Elephantine was located on an island in the Nile west of Syene, which is modern Aswan. These papyri prove that Elephantine was a Jewish military settlement populated by "Jewish soldiers." These soldiers guarded the southern border of Egypt, for this was the location of the first of the Nile rapids in the direction of Ethiopia. From this point northward there were no physical barriers along the Nile, which was the only axis of transportation between Upper and Lower Egypt. The Nile at this point is bounded by deserts making passage northward impossible. It was also a transit and customs station for the tropical produce coming from Ethiopia and Nubia, goods such as ivory, monkeys, wood, spices and gold.

The city of Syene in the land of Sinnim was built on the east bank of the Nile, in the vicinity of modern Aswan. The inhabitants of Syene, who were defended by the Jewish fortress of Elephantine, apparently engaged in irrigated agriculture. They may well have been employed in brokery and commerce with Ethiopia, transporting their wares along the Nile via the other Jewish settlements: Noph, Tahpanhes and Migdol mentioned in Jeremiah, en route for the Mediterranean countries and the Land of Israel.

The final question relates to the terming of the region "the land of Sinnim." Ben-Yehuda's dictionary defines *sin* as a tooth or a sharp protrusion. The meaning of the roots *sin*, *shen* and *zin* is a protruding object. This incidentally ties up with the meaning of Mount Sinai, which is a protruding mountain like the rocky crag, *shen haselah*, of Seneh and Bozez in Jonathan's war with the Philistines at Michmash (I Samuel 14:4). In Arabic the word *sin* has a similar meaning. In the wide section of the Nile at Syene, there are about a dozen islands built of rocks that protrude above the water, on one of which ancient Elephantine was built. These rocky islets, then, are the "Sinnim" mentioned in our chapter of the Bible, and the land of Sinnim lay within this fertile agricultural region.

DWELL AT MIGDOL, AND AT TAHPANHES, AND AT NOPH, AND IN THE COUNTRY OF PATHROS

(Jeremiah 44:1)

This chapter mentions some of the cities of Egypt inhabited by Jews:

> The word that came to Jeremiah concerning all the Jews which dwell in the land of Egypt, which dwell at Migdol, and at Tahpanhes, and at Noph, and in the country of Pathros.
>
> (Jeremiah 44:1)

We will classify the different functions of the cities, examine their location and discuss the activities of the Jews in Egypt. The country was divided into three regions: Lower Egypt of the delta, whose capitals were Zoan and Raamses; Middle Egypt at the apex of the delta, with the capitals of Moph or Noph and On; and Upper Egypt, or the land of Pathros, in the Nile valley, with the capital of No-amon. Three types of Egyptian cities are mentioned in the Bible: five capital cities and ritual centers such as Zoan or Tanis located at San el-Hagar on the Tanaitic arm of the Nile, Raamses at Qantir, some 23 miles (37 km) southeast of Zoan, which was built on the ruins of Avaris the Hyksos capital in the delta; Moph/Noph at Memphis, south of Cairo in Middle Egypt, and west of the Nile, and On at the apex of the Nile delta on its east bank; and No-amon in Upper Egypt at modern Luxor. The second group were border cities which served as military bases and customs stations for international trade, such as Sin, Migdol and Tahpanhes in northern Egypt, and Syene or Elephantine on the island near Aswan. The third category were the inner cities. Isaiah prophesies the following of the five capital cities:

> In that day shall five cities in the land of Egypt speak the language of Canaan, and swear to the LORD of hosts; one shall be called, The city of destruction.
>
> (Isaiah 19:18)

The town concerned is probably the city of Heres or the sun, at On. The prophets also proclaim:

> The princes of Zoan are become fools, the princes of Noph are deceived.
>
> (Isaiah 19:13)

> O thou daughter dwelling in Egypt, furnish thyself to go into captivity: for Noph shall be waste and desolate without an inhabitant.
>
> (Jeremiah 46:19)

> And I will set fire in Egypt: Sin shall have great pain, and No shall be rent asunder, and Noph shall have distresses daily.
>
> (Ezekiel 30:16)

The prophets also declaim against idol worship in the capitals:

> Behold, I will punish the multitude of No, and Pharaoh, and Egypt, with their gods. (Jeremiah 46:25)

THE NILE DELTA

> Thus saith the Lord GOD; I will also destroy the idols, and I will cause their images to cease out of Noph; and there shall be no more a prince of the land of Egyp: and I will a put fear in the land of Egypt.
>
> (Ezekiel 30:13)

On was the center of sun-worship, the sun being termed Ra in ancient Egyptian, or Beth-shemesh in Hebrew, or Heliopolis in Greek, and Jeremiah prophesies against this practice too:

> He shall break also the images of Bethshemesh, that is in the land of Egypt; and the houses of the gods of the Egyptians shall he burn with fire.
>
> (Jeremiah 43:13)

The identification of the cities is problematic, especially those in the north of the delta. Studies carried out by the geologists Niv and Friedman show that the northern part of the delta adjacent to the Mediterranean was inundated beneath the sea until the eighth to seventh centuries BCE, after which the region was elevated, and the city of "Sin, the stronghold of Egypt," or Pelusium, was founded there. This city, as well as Migdol, are mentioned in Ezekiel 30:15.

The cities listed in this chapter appear in order of their geographical location from north to south. The Migdol mentioned here is not identical to that found in the narrative of the Exodus from Egypt. The Bible and the Apocrypha mention 25 sites which are named Migdal or Migdol, and Gardiner points out that there were four places named Migdal in the delta. Jeremiah's Migdol has been located by scholars at Tell el-Heir, northeast of Qantara, and the archaeologist E. D. Oren discovered a fortified area extending over 10 acres, with a brick wall of 50 to 65 feet (15 to 20 m) to the north of Tell el-Heir. The ruins date from the beginning of the sixth century BCE and ended in destruction. The *tell* lies close to a canal drawn off the Wadi Tumeilat to the north of Sin and into the Mediterranean. Tahpanhes has been identified with Tell Dafna or the Hellenistic city of Daphnae, which was founded some 25 miles (40 km) southwest of Migdol near a canal drawn off the Pelusian branch of the Nile. Most of the remains date from the time of Psammetichus in the early part of the seventh century BCE. The military value of Tahpanhes is emphasized in Ezekiel's prophecy regarding the city:

> At Tehaphnehes also the day shall be darkened, when I shall break there the yokes of Egypt: and the pomp of her strength shall cease in her: as for her, a cloud shall cover her, and her daughters shall go into captivity.
>
> (Ezekiel 30:18)

Moph, or Noph, in Egyptian called Mahat Tawi, meaning "scales of the two countries," lay between Upper and Lower Egypt to the west of the Nile, 15.5 miles (25 km) southwest of Cairo. Moph was one of the early capitals of Egypt, and was situated at a considerable distance from Cairo so as to be away from the area covered by the Nile's floods. The capital city gradually moved northward from its original site at Memphis: first to Babylon, to Fostat, El-Askar and El-Qitai, and finally to modern Cairo, for the limit of the Nile's flooding was 2 miles (3 km) farther east in the fourteenth to eighth centuries BCE than it is today. No-amon, the Egyptian capital, was founded to the east of the Nile near Luxor, where the shrine to the god Amon was built at Karnak. This was the most magnificent shrine in Egypt, and included the city of the dead to the west of the Nile. No-amon was also of economic importance, since the gold mines lay to the east and south of it, and in view of its proximity to the Red Sea, spices and incense were imported by ship from Somalia by the kings of Egypt.

Hathoric capital in the open air museum of Memphis (photo Neithsabes, via Wikimedia Commons).

Pathros in Egyptian (*pa-ta-ra-si*) means "the southern land" between Egypt and Ethiopia (Isaiah 11:11). The Jewish colonies in these cities were probably based on the flourishing commerce of Tahpanhes and the capital of Noph, and from the time of Persian rule in Egypt, a Jewish border army was stationed in Migdol and Sin, the stronghold of Egypt, on the border of the Land of Israel. The Jewish force is also mentioned in Ezekiel at Syene, or on the island of Elephantine in the papyri of Elephantine, on the border of Nubia.

DEDAN AND TEMA

(Jeremiah 25:23)

This chapter mentions several desert kingdoms:

> Dedan, and Tema, and Buz, and that are in the utmost corners.
>
> (Jeremiah 25:23)

We may ask what these kingdoms were, where they were located and what were the occupations of their inhabitants. All these kingdoms had one territorial feature in common; they were situated in the desert, as related in verse 24:

> All the kings of Arabia, and all the kings of the mingled people that dwell in the desert.
>
> (Jeremiah 25:24)

Hence these were nomadic peoples who lived in the wildernesses within the borders of Arabia. Ancient Arabia had several unique features: it was the largest desert kingdom in the Near East, since southern Yemen, which was ancient Sheba, is a monsoon region with rainy summers. The myrrh and frankincense trees grew there, serving as raw material for the spice industry with export to the countries of the Middle East. Arabia was built of very ancient rocks, and possessed mines of gold and precious stones of the highest quality in the Middle East, as well as ivory and ebony which were imported from Africa and used by the ancient kingdoms of the eastern Mediterranean. Arabia was the only country in

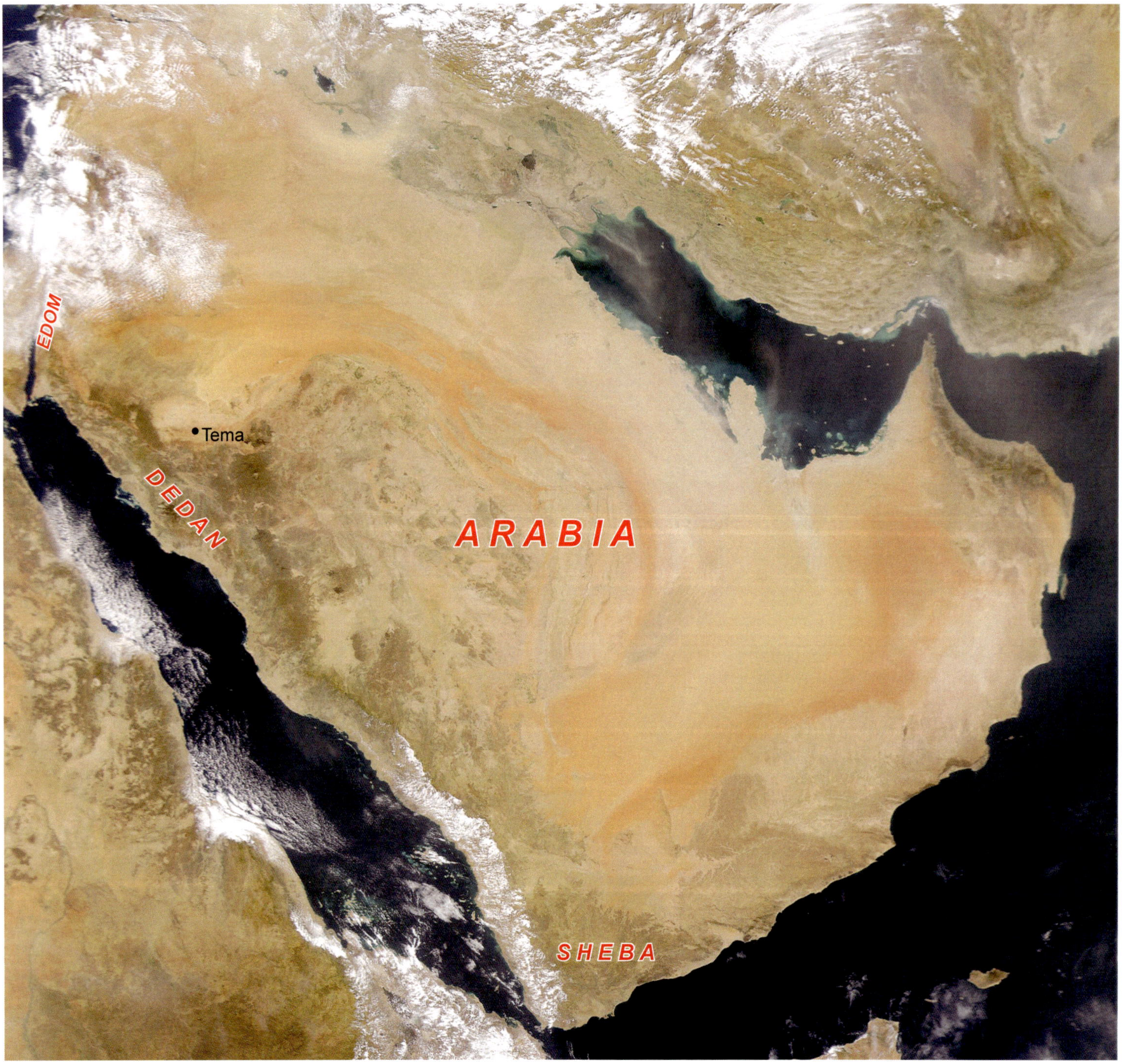

Satellite view of the Arabian Peninsula (photo SeaWiFS Project, NASA/Goddard Space Flight Center, and ORBIMAGE).

the Middle East whose whole economy was based on a single means of transportation—the camel. The camel was, in fact, domesticated in Arabia and Somalia, and the invention of the saddle made it possible to carry burdens over long distances in the desert. These luxury goods were transported from Marib, the capital of the kingdom of Sheba in southern Arabia, to the kingdom of Dedan in the north, which has been identified with the oasis of El-Awla near Madayin es-Salih in southern Midian. Isaiah has the following to say on this subject:

> he burden upon Arabia. In the forest in Arabia shall ye lodge, O ye travelling companies of Dedanim.
>
> (Isaiah 21:13)

The kingdom of Tema also lay in northeastern Arabia, and has been identified with modern Tema, about which Job said:

> The troops of Tema looked, the companies of Sheba waited for them.
>
> (Job 6:19)

The kingdom of Buz probably lay on the border of Edom, as we attempted to prove elsewhere, in our discussion on the place of residence of Job, since Job's neighbor Elihu was from Buz. "Those who have the hair of their temples clipped" probably referred to the relatives of the Kedemites, or a kingdom within the territory of the Kedemites, who lived in Wadi Sirhan to the east of Ammon and Moab, as described in Jeremiah 9:26:

> Egypt, and Judah, and Edom, and the children of Ammon, and Moab, and all that are in the utmost corners, that dwell in the wilderness: for all these nations are uncircumcised, and all the house of Israel are uncircumcised in the heart.
>
> (Jeremiah 9:26)

If we accept these locational identifications, we will find that there is some geographical order in the list of the kingdoms mentioned in our biblical passage, running from north to south—to the Euphrates, the Mediterranean countries and Egypt, each kingdom controlling one particular camel caravan route. Dedan lay along the Spice Route, leading from Sheba, the source of gold, frankincense and myrrh, along the longitudinal valleys to the east of the Hejaz mountains as far as Dedan. Dedan was the large commercial center, and the store for the distribution of the goods to Mesopotamia, Israel, Aram-damascus and Egypt.

> Sheba, and Dedan, and the merchants of Tarshish, with all the young lions thereof, shall say unto thee, Art thou come to take a spoil? hast thou gathered thy company to take a prey? to carry away silver and gold, to take away cattle and goods, to take a great spoil?
>
> (Ezekiel 38:13)

Tema was located in northeastern Dedan, on the route from the ancient port of Gerrha in Qatar on the Persian Gulf, where pearls were fished. This was also the port of arrival of luxury goods from India, which were transported to Hayil in the desert and to Tema. From here the goods were transported to Teman, one of the capital cities of Edom and to the Mediterranean countries. The food and water of Tema are described by Isaiah as follows:

> The inhabitants of the land of Tema brought water to him that was thirsty, they prevented with their bread him that fled.
>
> (Isaiah 21:14)

Buz apparently controlled the King's Highway in Edom, which branched out into the route to the Land of Israel, Egypt and Aram-damascus. "Those who have their hair clipped" controlled the road from the port of Gerrha via the oasis of El-Jouf to Wadi Sirhan, where the Kedemites and those with the clipped hair dwelt. This rift valley is 224 miles (360 km) long and 19 miles (30 km) wide and was the route followed by travelers to the Land of Israel and Damascus. Jeremiah prophesied the Babylonian conquests in chapter 49:32:

> And their camels shall be a booty, and the multitude of their cattle a spoil: and I will scatter into all winds them that are in the utmost corners; and I will bring their calamity from all sides thereof.
>
> (Jeremiah 49:32)

The camel was the only beast of burden used by these kingdoms. When it was first domesticated in the third millennium BCE, the camel was valued for its milk and wool. After the invention of the first primitive saddle which was made from four straps of camel's wool tied on to the hump, the people began to load their produce on its back and transport it over long distances. The prophet Ezekiel refers to these commercial peoples in 27:20:

> Dedan was thy merchant in precious clothes for chariots.
>
> (Ezekiel 27:20)

The passage refers to the woolen material tied onto the camel's hump to facilitate riding. There was constant competition between the two kingdoms through whose territories the routes passed, i.e., between Dedan which controlled the Spice Route, and Edom on the King's Highway, and the stronger of the two set the tone of trading in luxury goods from Africa, India and Arabia, as we find in Jeremiah 49:7–8, describing the downfall of Dedan:

> Concerning Edom, thus saith the LORD of hosts; Is wisdom no more in Teman? is counsel perished from the prudent? is their wisdom vanished?
>
> Flee ye, turn back, dwell deep, O inhabitants of Dedan; for I will bring the calamity of Esau upon him, the time that I will visit him.
>
> (Jeremiah 49:7–8)

THERE WAS A MAN IN THE LAND OF UZ WHOSE NAME WAS JOB

(Job 1:1)

There are differences of opinion among scholars regarding where Job and his friends lived. Some believe it was in northern Mesopotamia, or in the Bashan, in Damascus and Trachona, others identify it with Aram, and a minority believe it was in Edom. We feel that there is sufficient evidence suggesting that Job and his companions lived on the border of the land of Edom. The peaks of the mountains of Edom are plateaulike in structure, and they are built of limestone above layers of sandstone. The latter are the home of the iron, copper and other ores with which the mountains of Seir are endowed, and the crumbly soil is highly suitable for cultivation. The mountains are characterized by a desert landscape and climate, although they rise to over 5,580 feet (1,700 m) above sea level. The peaks attract humidity, so that some regions receive 20 inches (500 mm) of precipitation per annum in the form of rain and snow. Hence there are some localities which are covered by pine and oak forests (evidence of N. Glueck).

The plateau relief of the mountaintops, and their equable climatic conditions contributed to the development of a main routeway along the mountains of Edom, the King's Highway. The settlements of the mountains of Edom may be divided into three categories: agricultural settlements at the peaks, oases and shepherds' settlements on the eastern slope and scattered on the plateau, and the miners' villages in the western foothills.

Job's wealth may be correlated with the economic growth of Edom. This was a country with a varied economic base, including agricultural regions, mineral resources, and main commercial routes which provided means of livelihood and sources of wealth.

The agricultural zones of Edom are confined mainly to the rainy mountaintops and the terraced valleys which are watered by floodwater and are supplied with fresh water from springs. The lower parts of the eastern mountains, and particularly the western valley, are very hot and blasted by the east wind, and are hence unsuitable for cultivation. A vivid description of these conditions is found in Job 28:5:

> As for the earth, out of it cometh bread: and under it is turned up as it were fire.
>
> (Job 28:5)

Earlier, the narrative of Job mentions the feast held by his family:

> And there was a day when his sons and his daughters were

A camel amid the landscape of Wadi Rum in the biblical land of Edom, southern Jordan (photo Jorge Láscar, via Wikimedia Commons).

Nabatean remains of Petra (photo Brad Mering, via Wikimedia Commons)

eating and drinking wine in their eldest brother's house;

(Job 1:13)

We learn that vines were cultivated in Edom from another biblical reference in Isaiah 63:1–2:

Who is this that cometh from Edom, with dyed garments from Bozrah…

Wherefore art thou red in thine apparel, and thy garments like him that treadeth in the wine fat?

(Isaiah 63:1–2)

Similarly we find in Job 24:11:

Which make oil within their walls, and tread their winepresses, and suffer thirst.

(Job 24:11)

Professor N. Glueck discovered the remains of a prolific agricultural economy in Edom. He proved that the gods of the Nabateans were fertility idols, and that the most widespread motifs in both the architecture and drawings on the Nabatean pottery are those of vines and vine-leafs. Today, too, the villagers of Bozrah, Sila and Dana cultivate vines and other fruit trees.

The Book of Job states that he possessed:

seven thousand sheep, and three thousand camels, and five hundred yoke of oxen and five hundred sheasses,

(Job 1:3)

which were used mainly for ploughing, sowing grain and other farmyard tasks. This, too, correlates with conditions in the land of Edom.

Food was obviously a vital commodity which supplied the population of Edom and the inhabitants of the desert, whereas the metals and precious stones which lay beneath the rocks constituted the source of Edom's wealth. According to the research conducted by Glueck, the largest copper mines in the Arabah were found in Punon and Ge-harashim at the foot of the Edom mountains. Evidence of the existence of iron and copper in the land of Job is found in the following verses:

He shall flee from the iron weapon, and the bow of steel shall strike him through.

(Job 20:24)

Iron is taken out of the earth, and brass is molten out of the stone.

(Job 28:2)

Then shalt thou lay up gold as dust, and the gold of Ophir as the stones of the brooks.

(Job 22:24)

The sandstones of the Edom mountains were used as the raw material for glass and it may well be that same process was also used for gold, as we find in chapter 28:17:

The gold and the crystal cannot equal it: and the exchange

Camel with rider, relief from Tell Halaf (photo Walters Art Museum, Baltimore, via Wikimedia Commons).

of it shall not be for jewels of fine gold.

(Job 28:17)

In Wadi es-Sabra near Petra, remains of iron and copper mines were found, and above them was a forest whose trees supplied the fuel for smelting the ores.

The wealth of ancient nations was measured by their exploitation of raw materials and their commercial talent. The King's Highway passed through the mountains of Edom and was one of the most important trade routes in the ancient East with a vital junction for the caravans.

Ezekiel 27:20–22 states:

Dedan was thy merchant in precious clothes for chariots.

Arabia, and all the princes of Kedar, they occupied with thee in lambs, and rams, and goats: in these were they thy merchants.

The merchants of Sheba and Raamah, they were thy merchants: they occupied in thy fairs with chief of all spices, and with all precious stones, and gold.

(Ezekiel 27:20–22)

Similar evidence is found in the Song of Songs 4:16, Isaiah 60:6 and Jeremiah 6:20. These passages show that Arabia was the source of luxury goods in the ancient countries and Tema was the main commercial city of the region, as stated in Job 6:19:

The troops of Tema looked, the companies of Sheba waited for them.

(Job 6:19)

The large oasis of Tema lay near the King's Highway on the way from Mesopotamia and Damascus to Medina and Mecca, on the one hand, and on the route from the Red Sea to the Persian Gulf, on the other. The caravans used Tema as a station for obtaining food and water, as do the modern Bedouin to this day. We find evidence of this in Isaiah 21:13–14:

The burden upon Arabia. In the forest in Arabia shall ye lodge, O ye travelling companies of Dedanim.

The inhabitants of the land of Tema brought water to him that was thirsty, they prevented with their bread him that fled.

(Isaiah 21:13–14)

Obviously the trading caravans and travelers in the land of the Kedemites could not have existed without the camel, which was the "ship of the desert" and the only animal that could travel long distances in the desert, as mentioned in Isaiah 60:6:

The multitude of camels shall thee, the dromedaries of Midian and Ephah; all they from Sheba shall come: they shall bring gold and incense;

(Isaiah 60:6)

It is true that it was said of Job in chapter 1:3 that "This man was the greatest of all the men of the east," but his riches were probably similar to those of the other Kedemite princes whose wealth derived from the commerce of the King's Highway.

In conclusion we must point out that it is not enough to rely solely on literary evidence to determine the location of Job's country, and that geographical factors must be considered. There is no territory to the east of the Jordan so well suited to the conditions of Job's country as Edom. This region included both fertile and desert zones, for Job had hundreds of pairs of oxen and asses for plowing and sowing, as well as thousands of head of sheep at the oases. The Edom mountains were the only ones on the east bank of the Jordan containing mineral resources and precious stones. The mountains of Edom were the only ones linking the two seas over which the trade in luxury articles was conducted in ancient times. Mount Seir acted as a bridge between the regions of Arabia and Aram-damascus and Mesopotamia along the King's Highway. Thus Job was the owner of three thousand camels as beasts of burden in the desert, which was the secret of his wealth. His home was on the King's Highway near the mines, and as the Bible tells us, "This man was the greatest of all the people in the East."

I WILL DELIVER THEE TO THE MEN OF THE EAST FOR A POSSESSION

(Ezekiel 25:4)

Verses 4 and 5 of this chapter deal with the Kedemites who lived in encampments and fought against the Ammonites on their camels. We will now discuss their way of life, their dwellings and how they waged war against their enemies.

The Kedemites, who were nomads, probably originated in Wadi Sirhan in the Arabian peninsula. Numerous nomadic groups migrated from there to the eastern Mediterranean. They reared livestock and were engaged in seasonal agriculture. The nomadic herdsman is dependent on his animals which, in turn, rely on pastures and the shepherd for their well-being. Although he may cultivate some crops, the nomad is not tied to a particular territory and hence migrates from place to place, whereas the farmer is tied to his land where he must settle permanently.

The life of the nomad in Arabia is governed by a classic cycle. The hill country of Yemen is the only region in Arabia where it is possible to cultivate crops without irrigation because of the seasonal monsoon. When the population of Yemen increased, some of the herdsmen migrated to the wildernesses. Thus some of them became dependent on cattle raising. But the nomads maintained their connections with the oasis dwellers, with whom they engaged in trade in their surplus animal products, and from whom they purchased grain and dates. The nomad had to migrate northward to the cultivated lands of Mesopotamia and westward to the Mediterranean. This process took many centuries, and the nomads took to robbery, were involved in wars and alliances, sought refuge and made territorial conquests. On their wanderings they found places of refuge on the way to the Land of Israel and Mesopotamia. Here again they engaged in agricultural activities, first as salaried workers in the harvest season, and later to purchase land, as, in the Bible, Jacob did at Shechem. Here the cycle ends, but the links with the wilderness are maintained in the seasonal pastures.

Our verse describes the Kedemite nomads as dwelling in encampments. The encampment is a sort of temporary camp built by nomadic herdsmen. The inhabitants would pitch camp wherever there was an area of seasonal pasture, and in dry seasons would move to better grazing lands. The encampment dwellers usually lived on the borders of the ancient kingdoms. The camp was made up of tents and booths set up on a small hillock or a raised stone platform and it was frequently enclosed by a fence for penning in the flocks. In the Negeb and Moab remains have been found of rounded structures built of unhewn stone, with two or three rows on top of each other which may well have been the base on which the tents were pitched. This may be the origin of the *tira* (encampment), meaning lines of stones or a fence

THE ANCIENT NEAR EAST

"Thou art a swift dromedary traversing her ways" (Jeremiah 2:23) (photo vicharam, via Wikimedia Commons).

on which the tent or booth was set up. Psalm 69:25 shows parallelism between tents and encampments:

> Let their habitation be desolate; and let none dwell in their tents.
>
> (Psalm 69:25)

The life of the nomad leads to two other occupations: commerce and warfare. The encampment dwellers reared livestock and in very arid conditions, camels, which are desert creatures with minimal needs. Hence the natural occupation of these people was the transportation of commercial caravans on camels' backs. Since the nomads knew the desert and its sources of water, and since their camels rendered them mobile and they were acquainted with the other tribes and oasis populations, they could easily control commercial activities with security against the risks of robbery. Hence the Spice Route or King's Highway was used for the transportation of the trading caravans, as we find in Isaiah 30:6:

> They will carry their riches upon the shoulders of young asses, and their treasures upon the bunches of camels,
>
> (Isaiah 30:6)

or in chapter 60:6:

> The multitude of camels shall cover thee, the dromedaries of Midian and Ephah; all they from Sheba shall come: they shall bring gold and incense.
>
> (Isaiah 60:6)

With regard to warfare, the nomads controlled pasturelands over which they had rights, which were rigidly maintained as this was a question of life and death. For the nomad, pasture and water in the desert were of vital significance. Thus the nomads would gather together to make war on any other tribe that attempted to encroach on their pastures or water resources. When they became stronger, they would even invade cultivated regions or agricultural border cities, riding on their camels, as we find in our verse in Ezekiel 25:4:

> Therefore I will deliver thee to the men of the east for a possession, and they shall set their palaces in thee, and make their dwellings in thee: they shall eat thy fruit, and they shall drink thy milk.
>
> (Ezekiel 25:4)

AND SO IT WAS, WHEN ISRAEL HAD SOWN,THAT THE MIDIANITES CAME UP, AND THE AMALEKITES, AND THE CHILDREN OF THE EAST, EVEN THEY CAME UP AGAINST THEM

(Judges 6:3)

The origins of the Amalekites are listed in Genesis 36:12, where Amalek is mentioned as the son of Eliphaz and grandson of Esau. Verse 15 describes Amalek as one of the clans of Eliphaz in the land of Edom, indicating that the Amalekites originally lived in Edom. Other biblical sources, however, relate that Amalek did not live only in Edom and Arabia, but extended to the west side of the Jordan, as far as the Arabah and the south of Israel. In our opinion, the Amalekites controlled the main transportation axes of the region that they occupied. The limits of Amalekite expansion, according to biblical sources and geographical features, will be discussed forthwith.

According to Numbers 13:29, "Amalekites dwell in the land of the south." In I Samuel 15:7 we find that their territory had expanded during the time of Saul: "from Havilah as far as Shur, which is east of Egypt," which means from Edom to the border of Egypt. This process of expansion resulted in a war between the Israelites and the Amalekites at Rephidim (Exodus 17:8). The main base of the Amalekites in the Negeb was at Kadesh-barnea. From Numbers 13:29 and 14:45 we see that they lived both in the valleys and the uplands of the Negeb. Later on, during the time of David, the Amalekites made a base in the Judean Negeb (I Samuel 30) and they even penetrated the settlements of the north during the time of the Judges (Judges 12:15), reaching as far as Ephraim and the Jezreel Valley.

The occupations of the Amalekites were varied, including livestock rearing, agriculture and commercial activities. I Samuel 15:3 relates of the war between Saul and Amalek, stating that the property of the Amalekites included ox, sheep, camel and asses. In David's war with the Amalekites (I Samuel 30:2), the Bible describes the spoil of sheep and cattle taken by David. The livestock-rearing activity of the Amalekites hints at their cultivation of the soil, for Genesis 14:7 mentions "the country of the Amalekites," and we know that the term *sadeh* in Hebrew [field] refers to agricultural land. The Amalekites also owned camels, and in I Samuel 30:17 the Bible relates that four hundred Amalekite camel riders fled

Ein el-Qudeirat, identified as the site of Kadesh-barnea (Matson Photo Service, retrieved from the Library of Congress, https://www.loc.gov/item/mpc2010000406/PP/; accessed May 15, 2017).

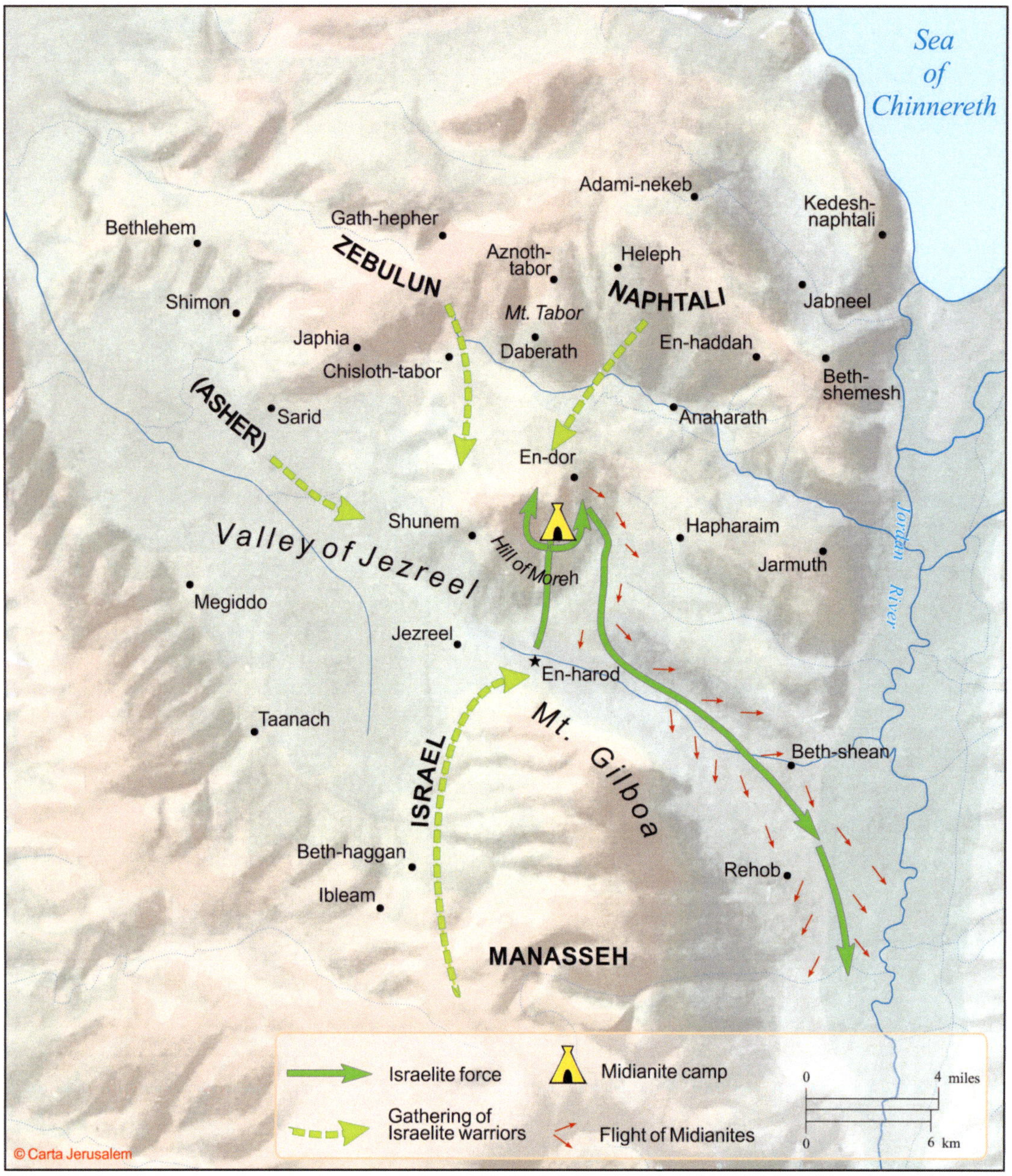

AND SO IT WAS, WHEN ISRAEL HAD SOWN,THAT THE MIDIANITES CAME UP, AND THE AMALEKITES, AND THE CHILDREN OF THE EAST, EVEN THEY CAME UP AGAINST THEM

(Judges 6:3)

from David. From these facts we may deduce that the most important occupation of the Amalekites was commerce, for they controlled the trade of their own country which was based on the King's Highway and also tried to gain control over the "Via Maris." The southern end of this road, "from Havilah to Shur," is mentioned in the war against Saul, and the other sections of it are mentioned in Judges 6:3–5:

> and so it was, when Israel had sown,that the Midianites came up, and the Amalekites, and the children of the east, even they came up against them;
>
> And they encamped against them, and destroyed the incense of the earth, till thou come unto Gaza, and left no sustenance for Israel, neither sheep, nor ox, nor ass.
>
> For they came up with their cattle and their tents, and they came as grasshoppers for multitude; for both they and their camels were without number.
>
> (Judges 6:3–5)

Thus it can be assumed that Amalek controlled the Jezreel Valley and the entire route to Gaza with their innumerable camels and it is also well-known that traders in ancient times needed a well-trained army to protect their caravans from robbery and pillage. The flight of four hundred camel riders from David is ample proof of the existence of a well-trained Amalekite army.

Hence we see that Amalek was a very large tribe extending over the lands of Egypt, Midian, Edom and Canaan, owning large flocks and controlling the trade routes. They also possessed a well-trained and organized army. We also think that the Amalekites controlled trade in the copper ores of the land of Edom and the Arabah, as well as the precious stones, gold and spices of Midian and Arabia and trade in the agricultural produce of Canaan and Egypt. Their advance into the Land of Israel was blocked by the establishment of the Israelite monarchy and when their power waned they retreated to the Egyptian border and their homeland in Edom. According to I Chronicles 4:43, the Simeonites fought Amalek during the reign of King Hezekiah of Judah, pushing them back from the Egyptian border and settling there instead. At this time it would seem that the Nabateans appeared on the stage of history, inherited the lands of the Amalekites on the east side of the Jordan, and gained control of the trade routes on either side of the river.

The war between the armies of Midian and Amalek and the men of Gideon in the Jezreel Valley took place at the height of Midianite power, since they had penetrated the King's Highway on the east side of the Jordan together with the Kedemites, while the Amalekites, who were also at their peak at this time, had invaded northern Israel along the ancient Via Maris.

FOR THE FIELDS OF HESHBON LANGUISH, AND THE VINE OF SIBMAH

(Isaiah 16:8–9)

Both Isaiah, in this chapter, and Jeremiah in chapter 48, prophecy the downfall of Moab, while Isaiah bemoans the loss of its agricultural produce:

> For the fields of Heshbon languish, and the vine of Sibmah: the lords of the heathen have broken down the principal plants thereof; they are come even unto Jazer, they wandered through the wilderness: her branches are stretched out, they are gone over the sea.
>
> Therefore I will bewail with the weeping of Jazer the vine of Sibmah: I will water thee with my tears, O Heshbon and Elealeh: for the shouting for the summer fruits and for thy harvest is fallen.
>
> (Isaiah 16:8–9)

In discussing the economy of Moab, we must first consider its climatic and geographical features. Moab extends to the east of the Dead Sea, between southern Gilead and northern Edom. Its southern border is demarcated by the deep Zered Valley which extends over 675 square miles (1,750 sq.km), and its northern boundary runs along the superficial valleys of the Heshbon and Nimrin rivers. The Arnon River, with a drainage basin extending over an area of 1,740 square miles (4,500 sq.km), dissects the central part of the land of Moab, and the towns of Dibon, Aroer and Jahaz were located in the ravines. Southern Moab rises to an altitude of 4,100 feet (1,250 m) above sea level near Kir-moab, its slopes are steep in the east, and even steeper to the west, and consequently the population there is sparse. Northeastern Moab is characterized by an extensive plateau with the lowest relief in eastern Transjordan from Gilead to Edom, its average altitude ranging from 2,300 to 2,625 feet (700 to 800 m). The plateau and the mountains to the west of it are densely populated, and include the towns of Heshbon and Medeba, Sibmah and Elealeh, Bezer and Kirjathaim. The steep mountain slopes on the western flank leave no coastal plain along the shore of the Dead Sea. As a result, there was no longitudinal route along the Dead Sea coast, and three

Canyon of the Arnon River (in Arabic, Wadi Mujib) (photo YousefTOmar, via Wikimedia Commons).

THE PENETRATION INTO TRANSJORDAN

(Numbers 20:14–21:30, 33:37–49)

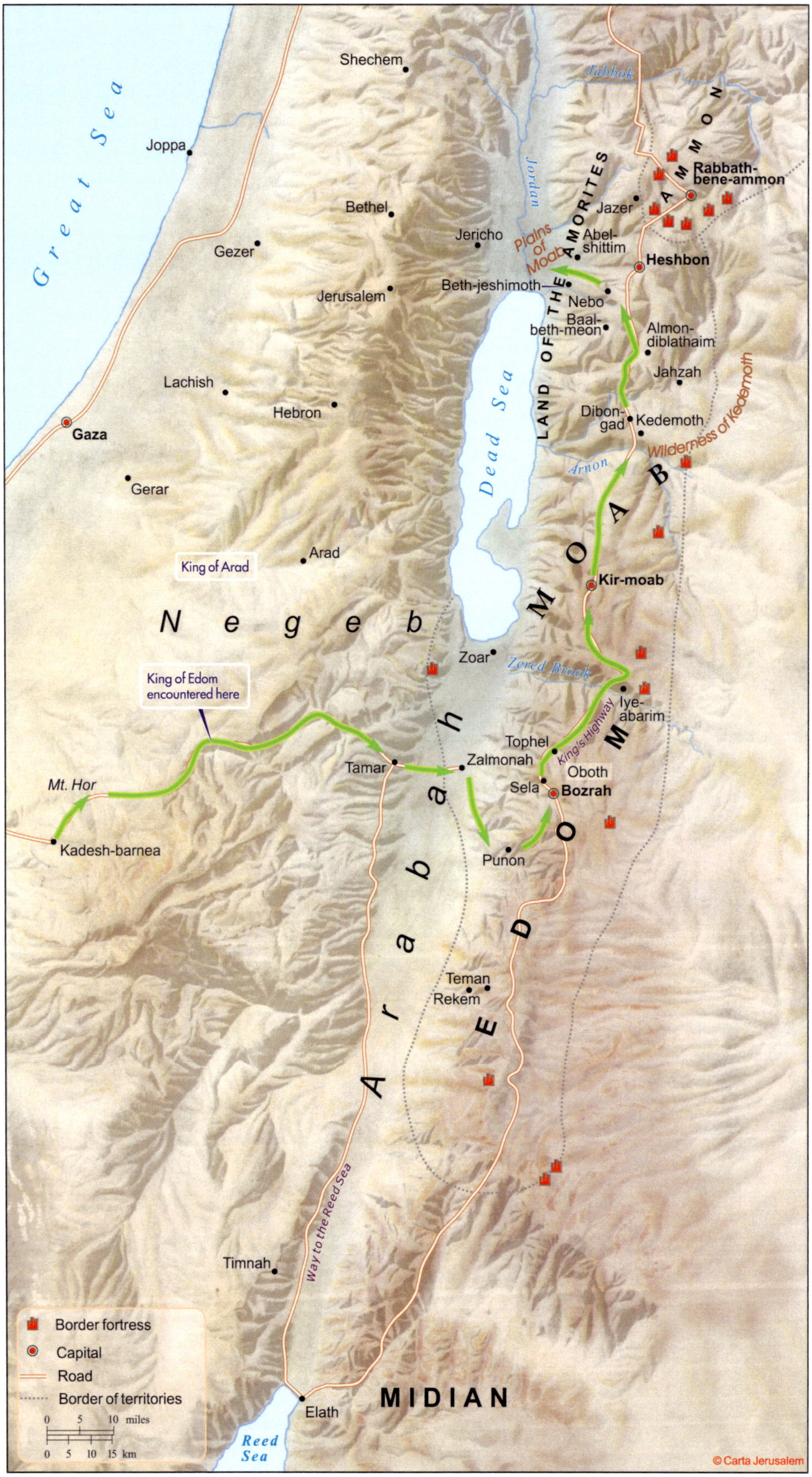

Aerial view of Heshbon (Tell Hesban), looking west (NEAEHL).

were set on the river estuaries: Arvot-moab in the north at the estuary of the Heshbon and Nimrin rivers, Arvot En-eglaim at the mouth of the Kerak, and Kikar-zoar and Amorah at the mouth of the Zered. Since the plateau of Heshbon is the lowest area in the mountains of Moab, it was the location of an important junction: *eastward* to Wadi Sirhan and Karkor in the territory of the Kedemites, Amalekites and Midianites, and farther on to the big oasis of Dumah and the kingdoms of Babylon and Sheba in the south; *northward* to Rabbath-ammon and Damascus because of Moab's links with Aram (Numbers 23:7); and finally *southward* to Dibon, Kir-moab and the Dead Sea, since the king of Moab constructed a routeway from Dibon to the fords of the Arnon (Isaiah 16:2), as stated in the Mesha Stone: "I built the road to Arnon."

The gold, incense and spices of Sheba were exported to Damascus and the Mediterranean and so most of the Moabite fortresses were constructed along this route (Jeremiah 48:18–19, 48:41). At its peak, the kingdom of Moab extended as far as the Heshbon Valley in the north, and was 56 miles (90 km) in length, and at its wane was reduced to 34 miles (55 km), to the Arnon Valley (Numbers 21). Moab's economic significance lay in the plateau of Heshbon–Medeba which was the grainstore of the mountains of Israel, together with Hauran. Our chapter describes "the fields of Heshbon," and several biblical references relate to the "plain of Moab" which extends over a width of 12.5 miles (20 km): "the Tableland" (Deuteronomy 4.43; Jeremiah 48:21; Joshua 13:9) and "the cities of the Tableland" (Deuteronomy 3:10; Joshua 13:17, 13:21). Thus we see that this was *the* classic tableland of the Land of Israel, with the exception of the Bashan. Further evidence is found in the migration of Elimelech and Naomi, during the period of drought and famine, from Bethlehem in Judah "into the country of Moab" (Ruth 1:2). The explanation of the absence of famine in Moab as compared with Judah is given by D. Ashbel, who has shown that the west-westerly winds which blow from the Mediterranean in the winter, precipitate rain in the Judean Hills and as they continue over the Dead Sea, become further saturated with moisture which is later deposited as rain in the plains of Moab. Evidence that grain was grown in Moab is found in Ezekiel 27:17, where the prophet relates that wheat from Minnith in Moab was exported to the kingdom of Tyre:

> Judah and the land of Israel they were thy merchants: they traded in thy market wheat of Minnith, and Pannang, and honey, and oil, and balm.
>
> (Ezekiel 27:17)

Heshbon, which was situated at an altitude of 2,867 feet (874 m) above sea level, lay between the plateau in the east and the mountains in the west and functioned as the chief city of northern Moab and the capital of King Sihon of the Amorites (Numbers 21:26–27; Deuteronomy 2:26; Joshua 9:10, 12:5). Heshbon was also situated on the border of the Reubenites in the south and the Gadites in the north. The Song of Songs (7:4) describes its importance:

> Thine eyes like the fishpools in Heshbon,
> by the gate of Bath-rabbim.
>
> (Song of Songs 7:4)

Only a very important and wealthy city had more than one pool, and Bath-rabbim (literally, daughter of many) probably means a city with a large population. Hence Heshbon was the economic center of Moab, lying on the international road junction and on the border between the cereal area in the east and the vineyard zone of the western, wetter mountains where the Sibmah of our chapter was located. The towns of Abel-keramin and Minnith, mentioned in Judges 11:33, were also located in the western part of Moab. N. Glueck has identified Sibmah with Qurn el-Kibsh, at an altitude of 2,660 feet (810 m), overlooking Wadi Salma which drains into the Heshbon Valley, and which is surrounded by a wall 984 feet long by 328 feet wide (300 by 100 m).

Cattle were raised in the river estuaries of Moab and the swampy regions of Egypt, as suggested by the name "En-eglaim" (*egel* = calf) located in this region, mentioned in Ezekiel 47:10. Professor Y. Yadin also discovered a document in the Cave of the Letters bearing the name "Eglathain." Further, the plains of Sodom and Gomorrah are often compared to the land of Egypt, as we find in Genesis 13:10:

> even as the garden of the Lord, like the land of Egypt, as thou comest unto Zoar;
>
> (Genesis 13:10)

Jeremiah, on the other hand, defines Egypt as "a beautiful heifer" (46:20) because of the large herds of cattle reared in the Nile swamps. The plains of Moab were probably a region of palm and spice cultivation employing irrigated methods, such as at Ramatha. The uplands of southern Moab were the cradle of high-quality sheep, for the Reubenites and the Gadites wandered in a "place [that] was a place for cattle" (Numbers 32:1), and in "cattle country," and the Bible relates that King Mesha of Moab was a herdsman, rearing stud rams:

> and rendered unto the king of Israel an hundred thousand lambs, and an hundred thousand rams, with the wool.
>
> (II Kings 3:4)

It would seem, then, that the wilderness of Kedemoth (Deuteronomy 2:26) to the east of Moab and near Wadi Sirhan, was the origin of the Kedemites who reared camels, for there were links between Midian, Amalek and Moab (Numbers 22:7; Judges 3:13). The Bible also states that "their camels could not be counted" (Judges 6:5) with reference to the wars of Midian, Amalek and the Kedemites against the Israelites under Gideon. On the other hand, these same peoples are referred to as nomadic tent-dwellers, and they are joined by the Moabites in this definition by the psalmist in chapter 83:6:

> The tabernacles of Edom, and the Ishmaelites; of Moab, and the Hagarenes.
>
> (Psalms 83:6)